COLWALL

Edited by James P. Bowen and Alex Craven
with Jonathan Comber, Keith Ray and David Whitehead

First Published 2020

A Victoria County History publication for the Institute of Historical Research

© The University of London, 2020

ISBN 978 1 912702 07 7

Cover image: *Harvest 1939.* The painting by Dame Laura Knight shows Kitty an old pony, and two donkeys owned by Alice Betteridge, stood looking from the Malvern Hills over Colwall towards the Welsh Hills. The two people seated on the ground are Professor J. R. Allardyce Nicoll (1894–1976) and his wife, Josephine. He was a British literary scholar, university academic and theatre historian. (Adelaide Art Gallery South Australia)

Back cover image: Colwall shown on John Speed's, *Herefordshire described with the true plot of the citie Hereford as alsoe the armes of thos Nobles that have bene intituled with that Dignitye, 1610.* (British Library, Maps C.7.c.20.(2.), f.49)

Typeset in Minion Pro by Jessica Davies Porter

CONTENTS

LIST OF ILLUSTRATIONS

LIST OF MAPS AND TABLES

Maps were drawn by Geoff Gwatkin, based upon drafts by James P. Bowen and Janet Cooper. (© University of London)

Map

Table

FOREWORD

COLWALL PARISH STRETCHES DOWN THE western slopes of the Malvern Hills below the dominating Iron Age British Camp, or Herefordshire Beacon, which is its most famous and important monument. From the top of this massive hill fort an exhilarating view of the landscape of hedged fields, cottages and small housing estates can be surveyed. Colwall is an unusual Herefordshire parish in that its population has grown substantially since the mid 19th century. This is partly because of its proximity to the important spa resorts of Malvern Wells, West Malvern and Great Malvern and also because it has own railway station. Like many Herefordshire parishes it has a wonderful range of timber-framed cottages, farmhouses and barns, and a medieval church. Several fine Arts and Crafts villas and houses from the late 19th and early years of the 20th century complement these earlier buildings.

This history of Colwall is one of a series of parish histories published by the Victoria County History (VCH) founded in 1899 as a national project to write the history of every English county. The aim of the parish histories is to publish local research as swiftly as possible and to inspire and encourage readers to become involved with the VCH in other parishes too. The Trust for the Victoria County of Herefordshire has published histories of Eastnor (2013) and Bosbury (2016) and the history of Cradley is currently being written.

The writing of this history of Colwall, like most such histories, has been very much a collaborative effort. Special thanks must be given to James P. Bowen and Alex Craven for their thorough and careful editorial work, and to the many volunteers and other people who have contributed to the volume and who are listed in the Acknowledgments. This beautifully illustrated book provides a welcome account of the landscape, social, economic and religious history of the parish and at the same time celebrates the landscape with which poets and artists such as Elizabeth Barrett Browning and Dame Laura Knight had such strong associations.

CHARLES WATKINS

Colwall Village Society

Revealing Our Heritage

Published with the generous support of
a grant from the
Geoffrey Walter Smith Fund
of the Woolhope Naturalists' Field Club

With thanks to the
Andrew Harris Trust

ACKNOWLEDGEMENTS

COLWALL IS THE THIRD PARISH history to be produced under the auspices of the Trust for the Victoria County History of Herefordshire. It continues the work on the Ledbury area which was started during the VCH-sponsored and Heritage Lottery Fund-supported *England's Past for Everyone* project. Like the history of Eastnor and Bosbury, published in 2013 and 2016, it will eventually form part of a VCH red book on Ledbury and the neighbouring Malvern Hills parishes.

The work of VCH Herefordshire has been supported by many donors, to all of whom we are extremely grateful. We should particularly like to thank our benefactors and subscribers who are listed on the donors page. The production of the Colwall history has been a team effort and the VCH Herefordshire volunteers with Dr Sylvia Pinches starting the research, Dr James P. Bowen produced the first complete draft which has then been revised by Dr Alex Craven with the assistance of Jonathan Comber who has handled the publication process from a Herefordshire perspective. Various volunteers have made major contributions to the research. Jonathan Comber wrote the sections on communications, modern settlement and local government. David Whitehead provided material on Colwall Park, Brand Lodge, agriculture and the church in the 19th century. Dr Edward Peters contributed the section on nonconformity and assisted with writing the entries for Brockbury Hall, Hope Pole and Joyces Cottage, Stone Holt, Cowlbarn Farm and Victoria Cottage. He also contributed material on farm buildings. Dr Jane Adams read and commented on a draft on springs and brooks and wrote the sections on the mineral water works, vinegar brewery and visitor economy. Dr John Fagg provided biographical information on celebrities and contributed material on retailing and highlighted the comparison of census figures for Colwall and neighbouring parishes. Gordon Wood shared his notes on railway history and the construction of the Malvern tunnels. Celia Kellett contributed to the research and writing of sections on occupations and hotels, inns and alehouses. She also undertook genealogical research for the landownership section. Penelope Farquhar-Oliver offered helpful guidance on historic maps particularly relating to Malvern Chase. Mark and Gillian Archer read and commented on the account of Perrycroft and C.F.A. Voysey. Dr Keith Ray researched and wrote the sections on Early Settlement, British Camp and the Herefordshire Beacon. Dr John Freeman has generously shared his notes taken from mainly medieval documents for his research on Herefordshire place-names for the English Place Names Society. Dr Della Hooke provided information on the derivation of Colwall. Professor Michael Rosenbaum, John Payne and Moira Jenkins contributed to the section on geology. Dr Lawrence Warner advised on the history of Piers Plowman, and Dr Mark Hailwood commented on a draft on the church house. Dr Sylvia Pinches, who carried out preliminary research on Colwall, commented on a draft on charities. Dr Sarah Ann

Robin commented on a draft of the section on the monstrous birth. George Demidowicz has shared the results of his research on the King's Chase and various buildings.

Colwall Orchard Group, in particular Wendy Thompson, undertook map regression analysis of the extent of orchards in the parish and we are grateful to Liam Delaney, Historic Environment Record Officer at Herefordshire Council for his assistance with Geographical Information Systems (GIS) and providing access to the Historic Environment Record (HER). Emily Lister revised the account of the Downs School and the Head teacher of Colwall Primary School checked the account of the school. John Eisel and Robin Riches read and commented on the account of the church bells. Dr Janet Cooper and Professor Charles Watkins provided much advice and feedback and offered valuable editorial experience acting as County Editors. Professor Christopher Dyer read the draft text, suggested corrections, and contributed at short notice sections on medieval tenant farming and the medieval social character.

We are grateful to John Croft, Chairman of The Trust of Dame Laura Knight for granting permission to use 'Harvest 1939' as the cover image. The British Library, The National Archives, The Royal Institute of British Architects, Lambeth Palace Library and Archive, Bodleian Library, Oxford and Historic England and Historic Environment Scotland have provided copies of images and granted permission for their inclusion as illustrations. We would like to thank the staff of the Herefordshire Archive Service and Herefordshire Libraries who have been extremely helpful and staff of the other archives record offices and libraries that have been consulted. We have also been granted access to the archives of Eastnor Castle, the Malvern Hills Conservators and the Colwall Village Society.

Finally, we would like to thank Dr Adam Chapman, Matt Bristow and Jessica Davies Porter of VCH Central Office at the Institute of Historical Research, University of London, for their work on the final editing of the book and seeing it through the press.

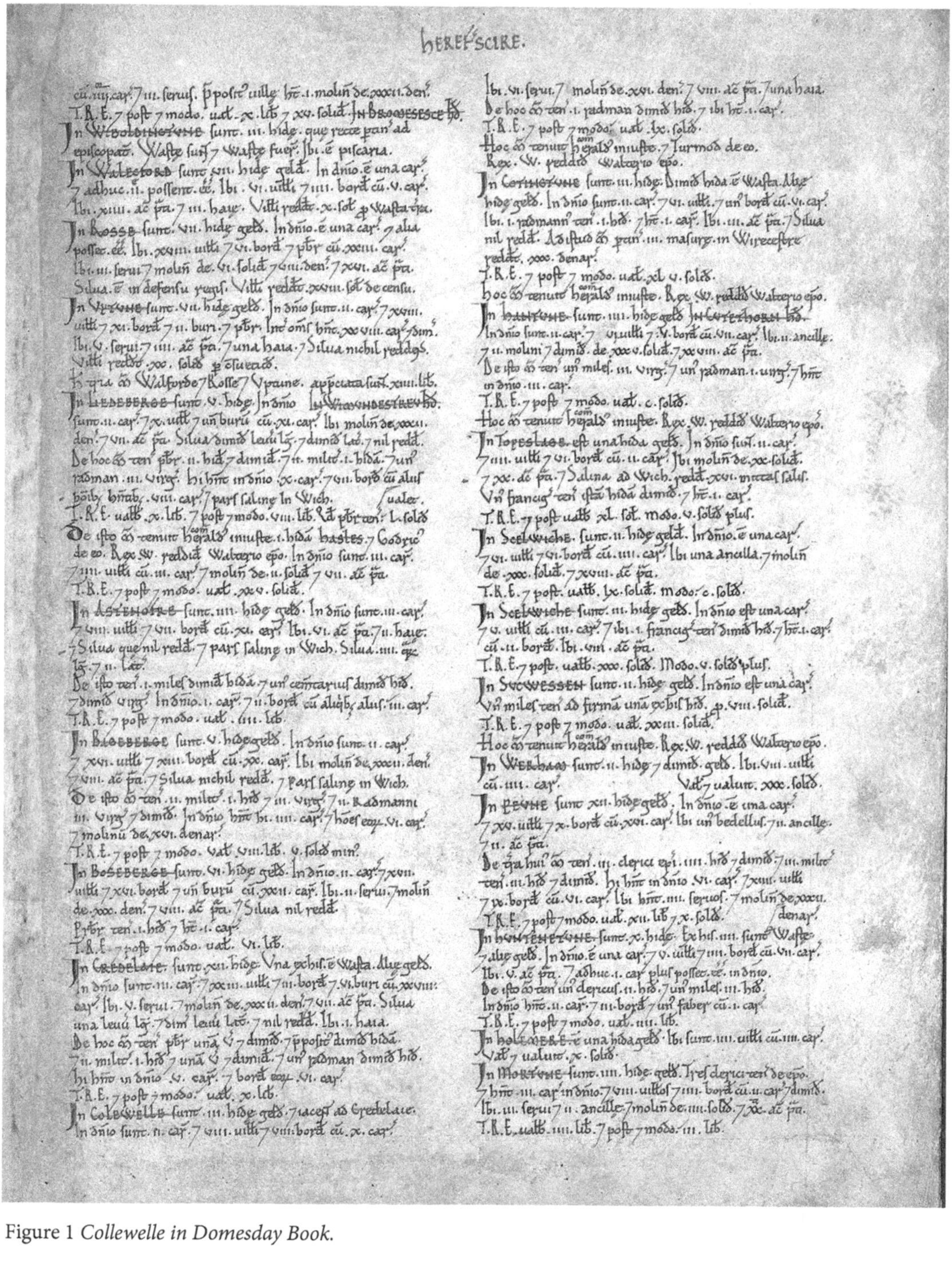

Figure 1 *Collewelle in Domesday Book.*

INTRODUCTION

COLWALL LIES 4 MILES (7 KM) north-east of Ledbury, and 15 miles (24 km) east of Hereford. The eastern end of the parish lies on the steep slopes of the Malvern Hills, where the parish boundary forms part of the border between Herefordshire and Worcestershire. The prominent Iron Age hill fort called British Camp lies in the south-eastern corner of the parish. Modern-day settlement within the parish is focused on Colwall Stone, a hamlet that grew up at a junction of field lanes with the road from Ledbury to the Wyche Cutting. The eponymous stone which stands in the middle of this junction is of uncertain origin,[1] but is said to have been brought in the late 18th century from a quarry near the Wyche to its present site, where an earlier stone may previously have stood.[2]

The bishops of Hereford were the principal landowners until 1868, although several other large estates have been built up since the 16th century. Until the 19th century Colwall's economy was predominantly agricultural, including the cultivation of fruit and hops. The construction of the railway station on the line between Hereford and Worcester, which passes through the Colwall tunnels, stimulated new settlement in the parish. The quality of the numerous springs which rise on the slopes of the Malverns has been appreciated since the 17th century, and commercial bottling of mineral water was an important industry in Colwall from the later 19th century until the closure of the bottling plant in 2010. Other industries were promoted locally by the prominent Ballard family, including a brickyard, vinegar brewery, ice works and fruit cannery.

The development of the spa attracted increasing numbers of people from the mid 19th century. The presence of artists and writers during the 20th century led to Colwall gaining a reputation as a cultural centre. It was suggested by Allan Heywood Bright of Barton Court in 1928 that the 14th-century poet William Langland, author of *The Vision of Piers Plowman*, was from Colwall.[3] Although the poem appears to describe the landscape of the Malvern Hills and a hill-top fortress corresponding with British Camp, few scholars give Bright's claims any credence. Nevertheless, the proposed association of Langland with Colwall persists.[4]

---

1   *PastScape*, no. 113829.
2   Below, Colwall Parish.
3   *ODNB*, s.v. Langland, William, poet (accessed 30 Sept. 2019).
4   See, for example, a plaque beside the car park at Wynd's Point.

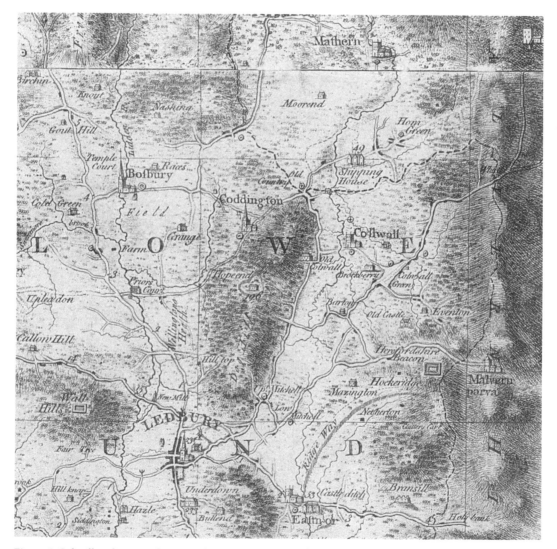

Figure 2 *Colwall and surrounding area shown on Isaac Taylor's* New Map of the County of Hereford.

COLWALL PARISH

Boundaries and Parish Origins

THE PARISH OF COLWALL WAS estimated to measure 3,800 a. in 1831, revised 20 years later to 3,771 a.[1] A detached portion of Coddington parish lying wholly within the boundaries of Colwall, was annexed to it by the Divided Parishes Act of 1882,[2] taking the total area of Colwall up to 3,835 a. (1,552 ha.) in 1891,[3] with broadly no subsequent changes.[4] The parish is long and rectilinear, measuring approximately 3 miles (4.8 km) in length and breadth.

The parish and its boundaries were surveyed by the Ordnance Survey in 1885.[5] Until 1897 its eastern and northern boundaries formed part of the county border with Worcestershire. The eastern boundary with Great Malvern (Worcs.) follows the Shire Ditch, running along the ridge of the Malvern Hills for much of its length. To the north the boundary follows a tributary of the Cradley brook, dividing it from West Malvern (Worcs.) and Mathon, which was transferred to Herefordshire in 1897.[6] The western boundary with Coddington parish follows the Cradley brook southwards from Colwall Mill Farm, before turning south-west to follow field boundaries to the west of Hope End, crossing a minor road to the east of Hope End Farm. The southern boundary with Ledbury and Wellington Heath, formerly part of Ledbury, follows field boundaries eastwards from south of Petty France Farm before meeting the Worcester road north of Massington farm in Ledbury parish. The boundary continues in an easterly direction at the Wellington inn, climbing back up the slopes of the Malvern Hills to meet the eastern boundary south of the Herefordshire Beacon.

Landscape

The spectacular ridge of the Malvern Hills which dominates the landscape of the area forms a wall running from north to south along the eastern boundary of Colwall, rising to a height of 338 m. at the Herefordshire Beacon, and 357 m. at Pinnacle Hill.[7] A ridge of high ground stretches westward along the southern boundary of the parish as it descends from the Herefordshire Beacon to the valley floor near Barton Farm. The western corner

1   Census, 1831, 1851.
2   HAS, AK40/44; R41/1; M5/44/17.
3   Census, 1891.
4   Census, 2011.
5   TNA, OS 27/2379; OS Map, 6" (1886 edn), Herefs. XXXVI.NW.
6   *VCH Worcs.* IV, 139.
7   OS Map, 1:25,000 (2000 edn), Explorer sheet 190.

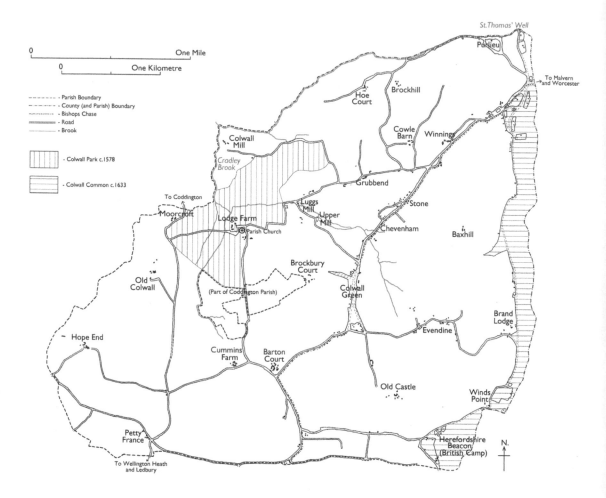

Map 1 *Colwall parish c.1842, showing streams and the principal houses.*

of the parish also lies on high ground, rising to 213 m. at Oyster Hill. The central belt of the parish is flatter and characterised by undulating lowland landscapes. Most of the valley land is above 100 m., although it falls below this level alongside the streams and brooks around Colwall parish church (98 m.) and along the Cradley brook (93 m.). The lower lying land in the parish is formed of acid loamy and clayey soils that are slowly permeable and seasonally wet. The higher ground in the east of the parish, including Colwall Stone, Upper Colwall and the steeply sloping hill sides, has slightly acid loamy and clayey soils with impeded drainage. In the west of the parish around Hope End the slightly acid loamy soils are freely draining.

The steep high ground of the Malvern Hills is formed of the Pre-Cambrian Malvern Complex rocks.[8] The western slopes of the Malverns are mainly composed of Coalbrookdale mudstone, into which narrow bands of Wyche sandstone and Wenlock

8   British Geological Survey, *Geology of Britain*, http://mapapps.bgs.ac.uk/geologyofbritain (accessed 18 May 2018).

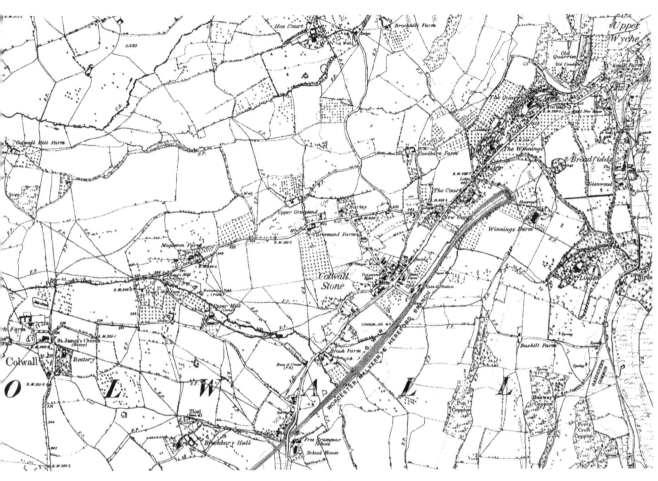

Figure 3 *Colwall shown on OS Map, 6" (1886 edn), Herefs. XXXVI.*

limestone have intruded. The sandstones and limestones, being more resistant to erosion, now stand up as ridges; the weaker shales and mudstones form the lower land between. Most of the ridges are broken by geological faults.[9] The fault line where the sandstone and limestone meets the granitic rocks of the Malvern Complex is pock-marked with numerous old quarries, and the limestone was prized in particular.[10] The high ground in the south and west of the parish is formed of Ludlow siltstone and mudstone, from which outcrop narrow ridges of Aymestry limestone. The flat lower-lying land of the centre of the parish lies upon Raglan mudstone, with some small patches of sandstone and limestone. Over these lie superficial deposits formed during the last ice age, largely deposits of clay, silt, sand and gravel which had flowed down the slopes into the valley floor. In the west of the parish, the diamicton of the Coddington Till is the remnants of the damming of the prehistoric Mathon river by glaciers. Between the two lies a narrow strip of alluvium deposited by the Cradley brook.

9   F. Raw, 'Structure and origin of the Malvern Hills', *Proceedings of the Geologists' Association*, 63 (1952), 227–39.
10   J. Barrett, *A Description of Malvern, and its Environs*, 2nd edn (Worcester, 1803), 16.

The name Colwall (*Colwelle*), meaning 'cold well' or 'spring', presumably refers to one of the numerous springs which rise within the parish.[11] Several yield the naturally pure water for which the Malvern Hills are famous, although others are saline.[12] The Pewtress Spring, a former source of commercially-bottled Malvern Water, lies on the north side of the Herefordshire Beacon, Evendine spring lies at the top of Evendine Lane, and the Royal Spring, the site of an early spa resort, is at the extreme north end of the parish.[13] Several brooks or rivulets run east–west from the springs to join the Cradley brook, which, rising just outside the southern parish boundary, flows north through Colwall and Mathon into Cradley parish, before ultimately draining into the river Teme near Worcester.[14]

During the Middle Ages the south-eastern part of the parish, approximately one-third of the total area, lay within the Bishop's Chase, a hunting ground belonging to the bishops of Hereford.[15] Claimed, presumably fictitiously, to have been established as early as the 7th century,[16] its boundaries were recorded in 1277 and 1577.[17] Encompassing the steep slopes of the Malvern Hills and the undulating lowlands at their feet, the chase stretched south from a point near the Wyche cutting extending across the boundary of Colwall into the parish of Eastnor. On the west the chase was bounded by the highway between Barton Court and the Wyche Cutting, and on the east by the Shire Ditch and Malvern Chase, the intercommoning of which by Colwall parishioners caused occasional disputes.[18] By the early 17th century the Bishop's Chase had shrunk to comprise only the uncultivated high ground along the ridge of the hills known as Colwall common, which in 1628 measured *c*.305 a.[19] Acquired by the Crown in 1559, the Bishop's Chase was disafforested with Malvern Chase by Charles I in 1632.[20] The Malvern Hills conservators were established in the late 19th century to preserve the natural beauty of the hills, and the district was placed within an Area of Outstanding Natural Beauty (AONB) in 1959.[21]

Communications

Roads and Bridges

An ancient ridgeway ran along the Shire Ditch for the length of the eastern parish boundary.[22] The main Ledbury–Great Malvern road (now the A449), which runs along

11   B. Coplestone-Crow, *Herefs. Place-Names* (Little Logaston, 2009), 70; *The Cambridge Dictionary of English Place-Names*, ed. V. Watts (Cambridge, 2004), 152.
12   E. Conder, 'The geology of Colwall District, with notes on the discovery of Brine', *TWNFC* (1898), 212–4; W. Wickham, 'On the Silurian salt spring at Colwall', *TWNFC*, 4 (1910), 293–5.
13   Below, Economic History.
14   HAS, CF50/243.
15   Below, Economic History.
16   *Reg. Trefnant*, 164–9.
17   HAS, AA59/A/1, p. 145; AA59/A/2, f. 103v.
18   Below, Economic History.
19   Society of Antiquaries of London, MS 520/VI/5 68.2.
20   *Cal. S.P. Dom.* 1631–3, 285.
21   Below, Local Government; https://www.malvernhillsaonb.org.uk/about-the-aonb/aonb-designation-and-purpose (accessed 6 June 2019).
22   G.B. Grundy, 'The ancient tracks and highways of Worcestershire and the Middle Severn Basin: Part III', *Archaeol. Jnl*, XCII (1937), 113.

the crest of a ridge between Chance's Pitch and Wynd's Point, is part of another ancient route.[23] As the road descends at Chance's Pitch, another branches off to the north, before leading in a north-easterly direction through Colwall Green and Colwall Stone towards the other principal crossing of the Malvern Hills at Wyche Cutting. The road through Wyche Cutting may have originated as part of a salt route from Droitwich (Worcs.) to South Wales.[24] Called 'Baldyate' in the 14th century and 'Baldenwyche' in 1582, the Wyche Cutting lay at the meeting point of the parishes of Colwall, Great Malvern and Hanley Castle (Worcs.).[25] The road between the Wyche and Barton Court dates from at least the late 13th century, with the section from Barton towards Ledbury referred to in 1324.[26] A map of 1633 depicted the 'Ledbury Way', running south-west from the Wyche Cutting along Stone Lane, and the 'Hereford Way', running west from Wynd's Point, both roads originating at Upton-upon-Severn (Worcs.). A third road, 'Bromyard Way', went from the Wyche Cutting down what is now the Purlieu, while a road originating in Cradley parish ran south along the western slopes of the Malvern Hills to meet the Hereford Way near the British Camp.[27] In 1796 the road through the Wyche Cutting was said to be too steep and uneven for regular use by carriages, but provided a short cut for travellers on horseback from Ledbury to Great Malvern and Worcester.[28]

Minor roads from Colwall Green, Colwall Stone, Barton Court, Cummins Farm, Petty France, and Coddington Cross converge on the parish church at Old Colwall. The road between Colwall church and Coddington Cross can be dated to 1300,[29] that between Barton Court and Cummins Farm was recorded in 1323.[30] A lane, little more than a track for much of its length in 2019, leads north from Old Church Road, between Colwall Stone and Lugg's Mill Farm, and then west to Colwall Mill Farm. Evendine Lane runs east from Colwall Green to Evendine Court, before climbing the slopes of the Malvern Hills and turning south to meet the main road at Wynd's Point. Minor roads lead out of the parish, from Colwall Stone north to Mathon, and from Petty France east to Wellington Heath, and south to Bradlow and Ledbury.

The road between Ledbury and the Wyche was turnpiked in 1721,[31] while the section from Upton-upon-Severn to Colwall was turnpiked in 1752.[32] A map of 1806 depicted the old turnpike road running between the Wyche and Colwall Green and then west from Cummins farm to a tollhouse north of Petty France. Another tollhouse stood at Chance's Pitch in 1806, on the road between Ledbury and Wynd's Point; it was relocated to its present site north of the lodge of Eastnor Castle in 1856.[33] Sections of road between Petty France and Chance's Pitch, and between Cummins farm and Wyche Cutting, were

23 Grundy, 'The ancient tracks of Worcestershire: III', 127–8.
24 Smith, *Malvern*, 3.
25 Smith, *Malvern*, 16, 22.
26 DCA 355; HAS, AA26/II/18.
27 Smith, *Malvern*, 168–70; WAAS, X705:24 BA81/366.
28 J. Barrett, *A Description of Malvern, and its environs* (Worcester, 1796), 49.
29 HAS, AA26/II/7.
30 HAS, AA26/II/15.
31 7 Geo. I c.3; HAS, BS96/46.
32 25 Geo. II c.56; HAS, CD1/3/2.
33 BA, 31965[STG]/97; M. Tonkin, 'Herefs. toll houses: then and now', *TWNFC* (1996), 429; NHLE, no. 1082151, Tollhouse Cottage (accessed 30 Sept. 2019).

turnpiked in 1832.[34] The turnpike trusts made few changes to the roads in Colwall. The gradient of the road from Little Malvern (Worcs.) to Wynd's Point was reduced and its corners widened between 1859 and 1865, generating complaints from the Hereford and Worcester mail coach that the works necessitated the use of additional horses to ascend the hill. These works were undertaken by Daniel Johnson, owner of Wynd's Point House, often against the wishes of the turnpike trust.[35] The roads were disturnpiked in 1870 and 1871.[36] The Malvern Hills conservators constructed Jubilee Drive, connecting the Wyche with British Camp, with public subscriptions to mark Queen Victoria's Golden Jubilee in 1887.[37] It was maintained by the conservators until adopted by Ledbury Rural District Council in 1924, although widening work had been partly funded by the council in 1897.[38] Ledbury highway board made several applications to make the road through the Wyche Cutting a main road in the 1880s and 1890s, finally succeeding in 1898.[39] Improvement works were made to it in 1954, which included slightly changing its route.[40]

In 1838 five bridges were reported in the parish surveyors' report, with bridges near Brockhill and Moorcroft being jointly maintained with Mathon and Coddington respectively.[41] In 1869 the bridge at Brockhill was repaired with contributions from both Mathon and Colwall.[42] In 1902 the Great Western Railway raised the railway bridge at Colwall by six inches.[43] Structural problems necessitated the temporary closure of the road bridge over the railway in 2007, and it was replaced in 2009.[44] The bridge at Brook Farm had been designated a County Bridge by 1899.[45]

Railways

The Worcester & Hereford Railway was incorporated in 1852 with plans to build a railway line along a route that would pass through Colwall.[46] A tunnel underneath the Malvern Hills was constructed between 1854 and 1861,[47] and the line between the tunnel and Ledbury was completed by Thomas Brassey and the Colwall-based engineer Stephen Ballard between 1859 and 1861,[48] when it opened to passengers. The railway was amalgamated with other local companies in 1860 to become the West Midland Railway, which was itself amalgamated with the Great Western Railway in 1863.[49]

---

34   HAS, C081.
35   WAAS, b705:583 BA707 D, 335ff; b705:583 BA707 E, 2-299.
36   WAAS, b705:583 BA707 E, 430: 33 & 34 Vic. c.73; 34 & 36 Vic. c.115.
37   HAS, AA86/3, p. 57.
38   MHC minute book, 1923–8, p. 46; HAS, K41/4, p. 11.
39   HAS, K41/2, pp. 173, 301, 337-8, 354; K41/3, p. 79; K41/4, pp. 70, 103.
40   HAS, BW15/13/4, p. 43.
41   HAS, CK23/44, p. 356.
42   HAS, K41/1, p. 139.
43   HAS, K41/1, p. 211; K41/4, p. 303.
44   https://www.networkrailmediacentre.co.uk/news/colwall-bridge-reopens (accessed 8 June 2019).
45   HAS, K41/4, p. 99.
46   16 & 17 Vic. c.clxxxiv; C.R. Clinker, *History of the Great Western Railway* (1964 edn), I, 282–3; A. Jowett, *Railway Atlas of Great Britain and Ireland* (Wellingborough, 1989), 80.
47   *Heref. Times*, 6 Apr. 1861; *Heref. Jnl*, 13 June 1855.
48   HAS, BG37/2.
49   Clinker, *History of the GWR*, I, 285, 290.

Figure 4 *Photograph of farm buildings at Colwall showing the spoil heap (on left above buildings) from shaft construction of the Colwall Tunnel, 1861.*

Figure 5
Photograph of the engineering staff of the contractors for Hereford and Worcester Railway: Brassey and Ballard, 1861 including Stephen Ballard in middle of bottom row.

Initially the line through Colwall was a single track, but it was doubled in 1868.[50] When the tunnel first opened for traffic in 1861, there were complaints about its low height and narrow width, poor ventilation, and steep gradient of 1 in 80. Concerns were raised about its safety when dislodged bricks fell from its lining, and in 1862 part of one of the three air shafts collapsed.[51] The safety of the tunnel remained a concern, and in 1907 its closure by a rockfall necessitated a replacement bus service between Malvern Wells and Colwall.[52] The original tunnel was replaced in 1926 by a new tunnel constructed parallel to it.[53]

From 1863 the station was served by three trains a day in each direction six days a week, with two services each way on Sundays.[54] By 1869 the number of services between Mondays and Saturdays had increased to four a day towards Hereford, and five a day towards Worcester, and by 1877 another passenger service towards Worcester had been added on weekdays.[55] By 1914 this had increased to eight passenger trains and two goods trains a day.[56] The goods yard at Colwall closed in November 1964,[57] the line was converted back to a single track in 1967,[58] and Colwall station was an unstaffed halt by the following year.[59] In 2019 there were regular services from Colwall to Hereford, Birmingham, Oxford, and London Paddington.

Post

A post office opened at Colwall Stone in 1844, renamed Colwall Green by 1857, and simply Colwall by 1891. In 1859 and 1876–7 letters were delivered by messenger from Great Malvern.[60] In 1886 the post office was near the railway bridge,[61] but by 1903 had moved to Colwall Stone. It closed in 2007, but reopened one year later in a former bank building on Walwyn Road; it remains open in 2019. There was another post office at Colwall Green from 1892 to 2000.[62]

A telegram office had opened at the post office by 1895, before which telegrams could be sent from the railway station.[63] A telephone exchange opened in 1898, but closed in 1921; a new exchange opened in 1940.[64] An automatic telephone exchange was built in

---

50   Clinker, *History of the GWR*, I, 289.
51   *Worcs. Chronicle*, 24 Sep. 1862.
52   C.J. Davis, *Round the Hills: an account of 70 years of Bus Services in the Malverns* (Bromley Common, 1979) 3.
53   Clinker, *History of the GWR*, I, 289.
54   *Worc. Jnl*, 31 Jan. 1863.
55   *Worc. Jnl*, 2 Jan. 1869, 30 June 1877.
56   *Great Western Railway Working Timetable*, 1914.
57   C.R. Clinker, *Clinker's Register of Closed Passenger Stations and Goods Depots in England, Scotland and Wales 1830–1977* (Bristol, 1978), 32.
58   V. Mitchell and K. Smith, *Worc. to Heref.* (Midhurst 1984).
59   HAS, BW15/3/8, p. 28.
60   *Slater's Dir.* (1859); *Littlebury's Dir.* (1876–7), 135; *Kelly's Dir.* (1891).
61   OS Map, 6" (1886 edn), Herefs. XXXVI.NW.
62   *UK Post Offices by County*, https://sites.google.com/site/ukpostofficesbycounty/home (accessed 18 May 2018).
63   *Kelly's Dir.* (1876–7, 1895).
64   Lists of Exchanges 1940, published by the Post Office in 1940; inf. from BT Archives, 20 Apr. 2017.

the 1970s near Walwyn Road.[65] Broadband internet access was available from March 2004.[66]

Carriers and Buses

In 1877 the carrier William Ireland ran a Saturday service to Worcester,[67] and in 1890 John Powell ran a service to Ledbury on Tuesdays and Malvern on Wednesdays and Saturdays. Members of the Powell family continued to operate carrier services in Colwall until at least 1912.[68]

A scheduled bus service began in 1911 with summer services between Great Malvern and British Camp via the Wyche Cutting, and a circular route from Great Malvern via West Malvern and the Wyche Cutting. In 1916 Midland Red commenced a weekly service from Ledbury to the Wyche, extended to Great Malvern from 1925; in 1922 the company added a service between Great Malvern and British Camp via Wyche Cutting. A service through Colwall between Hereford and Great Malvern ran between 1925 and 1968.[69]

In 1929 there were daily services between Great Malvern and Colwall, with services once a week to Ledbury and twice a week to Hereford.[70] In 2018, there were buses daily except Sundays between Ledbury and Great Malvern, stopping at Colwall Green, Colwall Stone and Upper Colwall.[71]

Population

There were eight villeins, eight bordars, a riding man (*radman*), and six slaves recorded in Colwall in 1086;[72] assuming an average household size of 4.5 for the tenants (not including the slaves), this suggests a population of 80–90. There were 77 tenants on the bishop's manor *c.*1288, which then included some tenants from Coddington but none from Barton.[73] The population is likely to have exceeded 350, and was then severely reduced in the 14th century, in which no doubt the Black Death played a part, as those paying the poll tax in 1377, 133 individuals over the age of 14, could imply a total of about 250.[74]

65   HAS, BW15/13/6, p. 1477.
66   *Sam Knows*, 'Colwall Exchange', https://www.samknows.com/broadband/exchange/WMCOL (accessed 18 May 2018).
67   *Littlebury's Dir.* (1876–7).
68   *Jakeman's Dir.* (1890 edn); J.B. Harrison, unpubl. paper on Ledbury carriers.
69   Davis, *Round the Hills*, 6, 11, 13–14, 31.
70   *Roadways Motor Coach and Motor Bus Timetables for England and Wales* (1929), 557, 571.
71   https://www.firstgroup.com/worcestershire/plan-journey/timetables/?source_id=2&service=675/676&routeid=19887461&operator=14&day=1 (accessed 18 May 2018).
72   *Domesday*, 502.
73   HAS, AA59/A/1, pp. 160–7.
74   *Poll Taxes* 1377–81, ed. Fenwick, pt 1, 358.

Table 1 *Population of four east Herefordshire parishes including Colwall, 1801–2011. Note: Colwall was affected by significant boundary changes 1881–1891. These figures are extracted from the published census reports, available at HARC, and data available through the Office for National Statistics (ONS).*

Year	Colwall		Coddington		Mathon		Cradley		Herefordshire	
	Pop.	Acreage	Pop.	Acreage	Pop.	Acreage	Pop.	Acreage	Pop.	Acreage
1801	635	3,771	194	1,076	547	3,366	1,317	5,966	88,436	534,823
1811	665	3,771	208	1,076	586	3,366	1,383	5,966	93,526	
1821	782	3,771	184	1,076	633	3,366	1,459	5,966	102,669	
1831	909	3,771	164	1,076	690	3,366	1,509	5,966	110,617	
1841	940	3,771	158	1,076	716	3,366	1,504	5,966	113,272	
1851	1,095	3,771	158	1,076	824	3,366	1,641	5,966	115,489	
1861	1,628	3,771	168	1,076	1,014	3,366	1,830	5,966		
1871	1,349	3,771	180	1,076	1,161	3,366	1,853	5,966	125,370	
1881	1,438	3,771	141	1,076	1,104	3,366	1,746	5,966	121,062	582,918
1891	1,506	3,835	168	1,028	379	3,038	1,189	6,075	114,404	
1901	1,892	3,835	144	1,028	387	3,038	1,194	5,783	114,125	538,924
1911	2,010	3,835	133	1,028	428	3,040	1,135	5,783	114,269	538,924
1921	2,043	3,835	147	1,028	410	3,040	1,113	5,783	113,189	538,924
1931	1,990	3,835	113	1,028	408	3,040	1,067	5,783	111,767	538,924
1951	2,066	3,835	112	1,028	402	3,040	1,162	5,783	127,159	538,924
1961	2,045	1,552 ha.	87	416 ha.	345	1,230 ha.	1,119	2,340 ha.	131,012	
1971	1,986	1,552 ha.	104	416 ha.	310	1,230 ha.	1,168	2,340 ha.	138,639	
1981	2,088		98		309		1,442		146,573	
1991	2,323		110		272		1,627		159,870	
2001	2,433		108		278		1,653		174,871	
2011	2,400	1,551 ha.	30		280	1,194 ha.	1,667	2,339 ha.	183,477	217,973 ha.

The first evidence for the comparative sizes of Colwall and Barton Colwall is supplied by the lay subsidies of 1524–5 and 1543–5. Eighteen individuals were assessed in Colwall in 1524, and 16 in Barton Colwall, suggesting a total population for the parish of over 200.[75] Sixty-six people were assessed for hearth tax in 1665; if they were all heads of households, and allowing for those exempted for poverty, the total population of the parish was probably over 300.[76] The Compton census of 1676 recorded 262 individuals over the age of 16 in the parish,[77] suggesting a total population of almost 400.

75   *Herefs. Taxes*, 67–8, 108, 110. For estimating the population, see N. Goose and A. Hinde, 'Estimating local population sizes at fixed points in time: part I—general principles', *Local Population Studies*, 77 (2006), 66–74; idem., 'Estimating local population sizes at fixed points in time: part II—specific sources', *Local Population Studies*, 78 (2007), 74–88.

76   HAS, AM29/1 TS, p. 70.

77   *Compton Census*, ed. A. Whiteman (1986), 260.

The population grew steadily over the 18th century, reaching 635 by 1801.[78] In 1831 Colwall had a population of 909,[79] and by 1841 this had increased to 940, including 20 persons 'camped in tents'.[80] Eleven people had emigrated since 31 December 1840.[81] Nevertheless, Colwall did not experience the rural depopulation seen at Coddington, Mathon and Cradley during the 19th and 20th centuries. The presence of railway labourers temporarily swelled the population to 1,628 in 1861, and it fell again to 1,349 in 1871. The population increased steadily to 2,043 in 1921, and it remained at a similar level until the end of the century, falling as low as 1,986 in 1971, before rising again to 2,074 ten years later.[82] In 1991 the population rose to 2,143, and it rose again to 2,433 in 2001 before falling to 2,400 exactly in 2011.[83]

Settlement

Prehistoric to Anglo-Saxon Settlement

The evidence of early settlement in what would become Colwall parish suggests that it was concentrated in the high ground of the north and west of the parish, and the low-lying central area, with no evidence of activity in the Malvern Hills before the Bronze Age. The earliest indication of human presence is presented by a Middle Palaeolithic flint hand-axe, a rare discovery for the area. It was found close to the boundary with Mathon, north-east of Hoe Farm, on what would have been high ground overlooking the Mathon river,[84] probably a camp-site occupied by early hunters.[85] Multiple finds of worked flints of likely Neolithic date have been recorded across the south- and east-facing slopes of the hill separating Colwall from Wellington Heath, extending from Old Colwall House to Hope End Farm,[86] indicating extensive activity overlooking the valley of the Cradley brook. Another concentration of worked Early Neolithic flint blades and debitage and a steeply-retouched Late Neolithic thumb-nail scraper, were found south of Colwall railway station. More flints were found in fields close enough to the Colwall Stone to suggest a connection between the two, perhaps indicating that the stone represents a vestige of monument-focused Neolithic activity in the area.[87] The flint finds lend possible substance to the story that an earlier stone occupied the site of the present somewhat truncated boulder.[88] A Late Neolithic square-butted flint axe, probably of Scandinavian origin, was found close to Colwall Tunnel in 1931.[89] A pair of tumuli, perhaps of the Early Bronze Age, lie 5 m. apart on the crest of the Malvern Hills at Pinnacle Hill, just

78   Census, 1801.
79   *A Topographical Dictionary of England*, ed. S. Lewis (1835).
80   Census, 1831; 1841.
81   Below, Social History.
82   Census, 1851; 1861; 1871; 1881; 1971; 1981.
83   Census, 1991; 2001; 2011.
84   Above, Colwall Parish.
85   HER, 2368; Pinches, *Ledbury: People and Parish*, 5; K. Ray, *Archaeology of Herefs.* 16–17.
86   HER, 3840–4; *PastScape*, no. 113877; PAS, WAW-569C21.
87   HER, 3833; Pinches, *Ledbury: People and Parish*, 8; Ray, *Archaeology of Herefs.* 81.
88   Alfred Watkins, *Old Straight Track* (Heref. 1912), 256; E.M Leather, *Folklore of Herefs.* (1925), 6.
89   HER, 3831; *PastScape*, no. 113801.

within the parish boundary.[90] The western scarp of the Shire Ditch, perhaps dating from the Middle Bronze Age,[91] cuts through the eastern side of both mounds.

Evidence of Iron Age settlement is principally focussed upon the spectacular hillfort known as British Camp, located on Herefordshire Beacon.[92] Settlements associated with the Camp and located on the valley floor may have enjoyed long continuity of occupation after the Iron Age. A cluster of Roman metalwork finds dispersed over a broad area c.1 km south of Colwall church may indicate one such settlement. These finds include at least nine copper alloy brooches dating from between 80 and 120 AD, and two Roman coins of the late 3rd century.[93] A similar settlement may have been found to the east of Colwall Green, where brooches of the same style and a characteristic copper-alloy narrow cosmetic mortar were found.[94] An urn containing 300 Roman coins of the 3rd and 4th centuries was found at Black Hill, near the eastern boundary of the modern parish.[95]

Archaeological evidence of Anglo-Saxon settlement is less forthcoming, but two copper-alloy strap-ends, from sword belts or harness straps belonging to high-status individuals of the late 8th century to the mid 10th century were found west of Colwall Green, as was a bronze strap fitting.[96] An 11th-century copper-alloy cast stirrup-strap mount was found north of Colwall Mill Farm.[97] A golden bejewelled coronet thought to date from the 10th century was said to have been found near Wynd's Point in 1650, but was sold and broken up.[98]

Medieval and Early Modern Settlement

Colwall, like other Herefordshire parishes, was a parish of hamlets and scattered farmsteads. Surnames recorded c.1288 included those derived from homesteads or settlements at the church and churchyard, Chevenham, Middleton, Old Colwall, the Sly, and Shirebourn, as well as landscape features such as a hill, a road, a valley (combe), and a well.[99] The hamlet of Shirebourn, where William of Shirebourn held a yardland by military service c.1288,[100] was occupied throughout the Middle Ages. Another two men surnamed Shirebourn witnessed a deed in the late 13th or early 14th century.[101] Thomas Caple of How Caple (d. 1489) owned a messuage, dovecote and lands there,[102] probably

90   HER, 3217–8; *PastScape*, no. 113797.
91   NHLE, no. 1003537, The Shire Ditch (accessed 30 Sept .2019).
92   Below, The British Camp.
93   PAS, brooches: WAW-FA4B2C, WAW-1781C2, WAW-34A317, WAW-9B53F1, WAW-6BFF95, WAW-6CC872, WAW-6BDBC8, WAW-6CB385, WAW-C5A6A8; pestle: WAW-6B0454; pin: WAW-DC01F9; coins: WAW-57D6D6, WAW-355A24.
94   PAS, brooches: WAW-94686B, WAW-2D0463; copper alloy mortar: WAW-2DDCF5.
95   Smith, *Malvern*, 10; 'Archaeological Intelligence', *Archaeol. Jnl*, IV (1847), 356–7.
96   PAS, strap-ends: WAW-55D482, WAW-0FE513; strap-fitting: WAW-6B9294. G. Thomas, Late Anglo-Saxon and Viking Age Strap Ends, 750–1000: Part 1 (Finds Research Group AD700–1700, Data Sheet 32, 2003).
97   PAS, WAW-7440D5.
98   HER 3830; *PastScape*, no. 113800; E. Lees, *TWNFC*, 2 (1867), 9; Smith, *Malvern*, 11.
99   HAS, AA59/A/1, pp. 160–6.
100 HAS, AA59/A/1, p. 161.
101 DCA 355.
102 *Cal. Inq. p.m. Hen. VII*, 1485–95, 190.

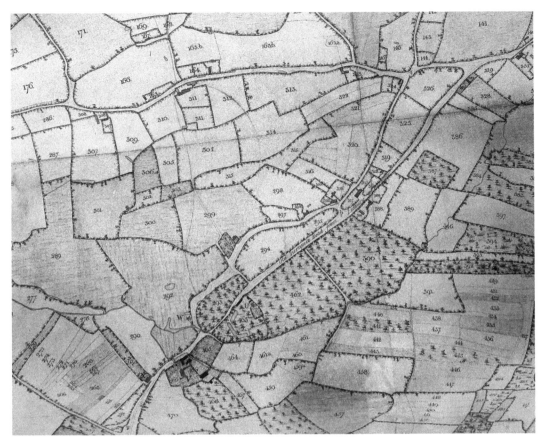

Figure 6 *Detail from the map of the estates of Lowbright and Richard Bright, depicting most of the parish of Colwall except those parts near to Hope End and Old Colwall House, surveyed by James Staples of Bristol in 1806.*

the estate of two messuages and arable lands which William Caple of How Caple had owned in 1412.[103] However, the messuage at Shirebourn had fallen down by 1577, and there is no later reference to the settlement, which probably lay near the northern parish boundary, on the stream called Shirebrook in 1577.[104]

Richard Smith of the Barton witnessed a deed in 1338,[105] and Thomas Smith of Barton confirmed a grant of land in Colwall in 1457.[106] The place-name Middleton, in or near Barton, was recorded in the later 13th century.[107] In 1321 a messuage containing two houses there, probably on the road from Barton towards the South field, was conveyed by one Smith to another.[108] The settlement may have been near the modern Cummins Farm, between Barton Court and Hope End.[109] Evendine was recorded as a surname in 1291.[110]

103 TNA, CP 25/1/83/52 (39).
104 HAS, AA59/A/2, ff. 63, 71v–74.
105 HAS, AA26/II/21.
106 HAS, AA26/II/36–7.
107 HAS, AA26/II/2–3.
108 HAS, AA26/II/9, 15.
109 HAS, L229.
110 DCA 2050.

In the early 14th century Richard and John of Evendine witnessed a deed.[111] Adam of Evendine occurs in 1321 and 1324, and William and Adam of Evendine in 1349.[112]

The antiquity of Brockbury and Cummins Farm is revealed by the remaining traces of moats that once surrounded them.[113] Although the present house dates largely from the 18th century,[114] Brockbury Hall was the centre of a medieval sub manor.[115] John Comyn held land at '*Rodyate*', near modern-day Cummins Farm, in 1272, and a messuage called '*Comynsplace*' was recorded in 1423;[116] it is possible that the priory of Great Malvern had an interest in the estate.[117] Oldcastle Farm has been suggested as a third possible moated site within the parish, but it is more likely that the pond north of the farmhouse is all that remains of a fishpond, of uncertain date.[118] The farm, which presumably takes its name from the nearby British Camp, was recorded in the late 16th century.[119] In 1671 it was occupied by the gentleman Rowland Pitt, and in 1686 it comprised a hall, parlour and dining room, four upstairs chambers and a cockloft, a dairy house, a buttery, and a kitchen.[120]

The parish church was presumably an early focus of settlement, and there are 16th-century houses on either side of the church. Evendine, which appears to lie at the centre of a field system revealed by remains of ridge and furrow and strip lynchets,[121] may have been another area of concentrated settlement, where several 16th- and 17th-century houses are extant. There are a number of isolated houses and cottages of the same period lining the road between Colwall Green and the Wyche Cutting, and the lane between Colwall Stone and the parish church. Isolated farmhouses, such as Cowlbarn farm and Brockhill farm, date from the 17th century, although these buildings may have replaced earlier structures on the same site. From the late 17th century onwards there was progressive encroachment onto the commons at Colwall Green and Upper Colwall. The numerous cottages with small, long and narrow gardens at either end of Colwall Green appear to have been intakes from the green.

Settlement from the 18th to 21st Centuries

Taylor's map of 1754 depicted the principal houses within the parish at Barton, Brockbury, Evendine, Hope End, Oldcastle, and Old Colwall.[122] A later edition also included the farms at Brockhill, Cowlbarn, Cummins, Grubend, Hoars, Lugg's Mill, Netherpath, and the Tanhouse, principal houses at the Court, the Lodge, Sly House, and Walwyn's Charity School.[123] When the parish was surveyed in 1812, and again in 1832,

---

111 HAS, AA26/II/5.
112 HAS, AA26/II/9, 18, 23.
113 HER, 3829, 3834, 3838; R. Shoesmith, *Castles and Moated Sites of Herefs.* (Little Logaston, 2009), 93–4.
114 NHLE, no. 1349730, Brockbury Hall (accessed 30 Sept. 2019).
115 Below, Landownership.
116 HAS, AA26/II/1; AE30/46.
117 HAS, AE30/471; *VCH Worcs.* II, 136–43.
118 HER, 3829.
119 TNA, PROB 11/79/102.
120 HAS, 94/1/30, will of Rowland Pitt, 1686.
121 *PastScape*, nos 1334810, 1334820, 1334826, 1334829.
122 Isaac Taylor, *This New Map of the County of Hereford* (Ross, 1754).
123 I. Taylor, *A New Map of Herefs. Etc.* (1786)

settlement still predominantly comprised a number of dispersed farms, with clusters of cottages at the southern end of Colwall Green and along Evendine Lane.[124]

The construction of the railway station stimulated development around Colwall Stone, and by the early 20th century it was the main settlement within the parish.[125] During the second half of the 19th century modern improvements such as piped water and gas were introduced to the parish. From 1866 Stephen Ballard used the Glenwood spring to supply the Winnings, Quarry House, and the Court; later he also used Pitts Spring near Chase Road.[126] A two-inch cast-iron water main was constructed from Glenwood, and reservoirs built to the south of the main road opposite the Winnings, to provide the village with a water supply. In 1891 the town of Malvern sought to take water from the west side of the Malvern Hills, but they were successfully opposed by the inhabitants of Colwall.[127] At the end of the century a reservoir was built in the north of the parish, across the boundary with Mathon, despite the opposition of Colwall parish council. Filter beds and a pumping station were built in Colwall, necessitating the diversion of the Purlieu, and conduits supplied water to Colwall, Mathon and Cradley, although Colwall inhabitants were still able to obtain water for their own use from springs within the parish.[128] By an Act of Parliament, the water mains were extended to most of Colwall parish in 1905.[129] A gas works was constructed near Mapleton farm at the end of the 19th century,[130] quickly supplying 100 customers within the parish, and gas lamps were also erected within the parish c.1900.[131] No development has occurred on the hills around Colwall since the Malvern Hills conservators were granted powers under the Malvern Hills Act of 1884 to prevent further development affecting the Hills.[132] Efforts by Herefordshire Council c.1970 to demolish houses on Beacon Road as not in character with the hills were defeated by local resistance.[133]

Development within the parish during the 20th century has predominately been in the area of Colwall Stone, comprising a mixture of houses built by the RDC and private developers. A racecourse was laid out to the east of the railway station in 1900,[134] and stables and other buildings associated with the course were erected to the south and east of Colwall Green soon afterwards.[135] Four council houses were erected at the eastern end of Mill Lane in 1919,[136] where St Crispin's Chapel and a church room were also built in 1927.[137] The water main was extended to the Downs School in 1920,[138] and 160 premises were connected to the water mains by 1925.[139] A group of council houses was erected

124 BL, OS Drawings, OSD 216; Eastnor Castle Archive, Map of Eastnor Estate, 1832.
125 OS Map, 6" (1905 edn), Herefs. XXXVI.NE.
126 Ballard, *Colwall Collection*, 57–60.
127 *Worc. Jnl,* 24 Jan. 1891; 54 & 55 Vic. c.xcvi.
128 WAAS, 493.22 BA9581/16.
129 5 Edw. VII c.clxxxiv.
130 OS Map, 6" (1905 edn), Herefs. XXXVI.NW & NE; below, Economic History.
131 HAS, T9/35–38.
132 47 & 48 Vic. c.clxxv.
133 *Malvern Gaz.* 3 Apr. 1969; 24 Apr. 1969; 20 Nov. 1969; 11 Dec. 1969; 15 Apr. 1970.
134 Below, Social History.
135 Below, built character.
136 HAS, BW15/3/7, p. 31.
137 Below, Religious History.
138 WAAS, 493 BA9196a/195.
139 Ballard, *Colwall Collection*, 59.

in Orlin Road c.1936,[140] and the Crescent had been laid out by 1938, by which time a number of buildings had also been built lining the east side of Walwyn Road.[141] To serve the growing community, electricity mains were laid by the Shropshire, Worcestershire and Staffordshire Electricity Company at least as far as the Elms School in 1931,[142] and the gas mains were extended to Upper Colwall, Evendine Corner, along Mathon Road, and to Barton Court c.1932.[143] Electricity cables were laid to Evendine in 1934, to the Purlieu and Lindens in 1935,[144] and to the Farm and British Legion Club in 1936, and more were planned for the Knell in 1937.[145] Nevertheless, with the exception of the large houses with working farms, most of the farms in Colwall were still not connected to the electricity mains by 1941, and many still drew their water from wells.[146] Electric power was extended to the Winnings and along Jubilee Drive in 1946,[147] when 87 electric street lamps were erected along the principal roads of the parish.[148]

Orlin Road was extended in 1949,[149] and seven houses and two bungalows had been built at Brookside by 1955.[150] Water mains were laid from the Wyche to Evendine in 1961, and along Mathon Road in 1962,[151] although as late as 1965 ten houses at Lugg's Mill were still not connected to the mains.[152] From the 1970s, development of the parish quickened in pace. Again, this has tended to focus upon Colwall Stone, although 23 houses were approved at Colwall Green in 1973.[153]

During the final three decades of the 20th century, there was significant development of the village either side of the Walwyn Road, beginning with an estate at Chevenham constructed by Malvern Hills district council,[154] and including private development at Pedlingham's Field,[155] and near Brook Farm.[156] Following the demolition of the former Coca-Cola-Schweppes bottling plant, construction began in 2014 of a small estate which would retain the tank house of the plant. Outside the village, 19th-century farm buildings at Barton Farm and Colwall Park Farm have been converted to dwellings.[157] At Upper Colwall six houses were built on a former builders' yard, and the Royal Wells Brewery site was converted into flats, both in 1997.[158]

---

140   Datestone on house.
141   OS Map, 6" (1948 edn), Worcs. XLVI.NE.
142   HAS, BW15/13/1, pp. 59, 64.
143   HAS, E77/4, 19 Feb. 1935.
144   HAS, BW15/13/1, pp. 279, 326.
145   HAS, BW15/13/2, pp. 7, 18, 30.
146   TNA, MAF 32/5/151.
147   HAS, BW15/13/2, 9 Jul. 1946; 3rd Sep. 1946.
148   HAS, T9/36.
149   HAS, BW15/13/2, 1 Oct. 1946; 18 Jan. 1949; BW15/13/3, p. 524.
150   HAS, BW15/13/4, p. 162.
151   WAAS, 493 BA9196/195a (xii).
152   HAS, BW15/13/6, p. 1221.
153   HAS, BW15/13/12, p. 25; CG36/2, p. 33.
154   HAS, CG 36/2, p. 97.
155   HAS, CG36/2, pp. 7, 30, 91, 125, 204; CG36/3, p. 5, CG36/6, 28 Aug. 1996.
156   WAAS, 592:01 BA14605, 22:1, 9 June 1997.
157   Brookes and Pevsner, Herefs. 177; HAS, L229.
158   MHC minute book, 1981–4, 126; WAAS, 805:876 BA8077, 50.

The Built Character

Like its neighbours, Colwall contains many timber-framed buildings erected in the 16th and 17th centuries, although many were altered and extended in later centuries. Few were very large, and of the 66 householders assessed for hearth tax in 1665, only 13 were assessed for more than two hearths.[159] The gentleman Maurice Berkeley and the yeoman Henry Wright both had eight hearths, and the manor house at Barton Colwall had six. Extant inventories reveal the contents of some late-17th-century buildings. The yeoman John Nelme lived in a house with a kitchen, a parlour, a buttery, a dayhouse, three upstairs bedchambers, and chambers for corn and cheese.[160] The inventory of John Unett named the hall and parlour, with chambers over them, two other little chambers, a cider house, and a deyhouse.[161] The glover Richard Pitt, who was assessed for two hearths, and William Hill both occupied houses comprising a hall and downstairs chamber with two chambers upstairs; Hill's inventory also refers to a corn chamber.[162]

A large proportion of the buildings in Colwall, particularly at Colwall Stone and Colwall Green, date from the late 19th and early 20th centuries. They are typically of red brick with slate roofs, sometimes with timber-framed gables, decorative tiling and polychrome brickwork. Some of the decorative bricks, such as those in Shelsley Lodge of 1893, were produced by Colwall brick and tile works.[163] The discovery of the spa waters at Malvern Wells in the mid 18th century had a considerable impact upon Upper Colwall, which was formed through a process of creeping suburbanisation from Colwall Stone towards Wyche Cutting. A new church was erected c.1909–10 to serve this growing community.[164] The Malvern Hills conservators laid out Jubilee Drive from Wyche Cutting to British Camp c.1887–9,[165] and several fine Arts and Crafts villas were built along its length.[166] The less developed area of the village, between Grovesend Farm and Upper Colwall, was designated a conservation area in 2001.[167]

Buildings Before 1800

Although several sites have been occupied continuously since the Middle Ages,[168] there are few recorded medieval elements among the extant buildings of the parish, although detailed investigation of individual properties might reveal more. Two buildings which may date from the late 15th century lying along Walwyn Road are Stone Holt, formerly Stone farm and named for the adjacent Colwall Stone, and Hope Pole Cottage. Both are timber-framed and comprise 1½ storeys, although this earlier construction has been obscured in both by later brick additions, which at Hope Pole Cottage now form a

159 HAS, AM29/1 TS, p. 70.
160 HAS, 126/6/10, will of John Nelme, 1697.
161 HAS, 26/2/40, will of John Unett, 1670.
162 HAS, 18/4/8, inventory of Richard Pitt, 1667; 13/2/21, will of William Hill, 1667.
163 Below, Economic History.
164 Below, Religious History.
165 Above, communications.
166 Smith, *Malvern*, 216, 235.
167 *London Gaz.* 24 Aug. 2001, p. 10060.
168 Above, settlement.

separate dwelling. Smoke blackening on roof timbers at both properties reveals that they were originally open-halled.[169]

Several of the timber-framed farmhouses of the parish, including Brockhill farm and Cowlbarn farm, certainly date from the early 17th century, and may contain much earlier material.[170] More buildings of this period lie on the lanes between Colwall Stone and the parish church, including Barn House, the Homestead, Mapleton, Peattys Cottage, Stamps Cottage, and Winterslow.[171] Church Cottage, formerly a church house,[172] and Park farm may both originally date from the 16th century.[173] Along the road between Colwall Stone and Colwall Green stand Bridge Cottage, Brook House, Fortey's Cottage, and High Gate, all dating from the 17th century.[174] The south-western approach to Colwall Green is flanked by a number of 17th- and 18th-century buildings, such as the Barton Cottages, Broadleigh, Netherpaths, Tan House Farm,[175] and the Yew Tree inn.[176] Several more 17th-century timber-framed buildings lie along Evendine Lane, running east from Colwall Green towards Wynd's Point, including the Hartlands, originally two cottages, the Malthouse, the Upper House, and two small thatched barns.[177]

Several large houses were built in the parish during the late 17th and 18th centuries. The timber-framed Oldcastle farm was built in the early 17th century and remodelled in the 18th.[178] Built on two storeys across four bays, it retains some original internal features, such as its 17th-century staircase. Petty France farmhouse probably dates from the 17th century, although much altered from the late 19th century.[179] Two storeys high and three bays wide, it is timber-framed with a rubble casing and had a thatched roof until 1939. Large houses were erected in the middle of the 18th century at Hoe Court, Hope End, and Old Colwall.[180]

Victorian and Edwardian Buildings

In 1851 there were 217 houses in the parish, rising to 299 in 1881, and 410 by 1901.[181] From the middle of the century, several grand villas were laid out along the main road

169 Brooks and Pevsner, *Herefs.* 178; NHLE, no. 1082123, Joyces and Hope Pole Cottage (accessed 30 Sept. 2019); James, 'Buildings 2014', 173–6.
170 NHLE, nos 1178833, High Gate; 1302288, Cowl Barn Farmhouse; 1349741, Brockhill Farmhouse (accessed 30 Sept. 2019).
171 NHLE, nos 1082158, Mapleton; 1178608, Stamps Cottage East and adjoining Cottage to W; 1178689, Peatys Cottage; 1302305, The Homestead and Attached Stable Block; 1349716, Barn House; 1349717, Winterslow (accessed 30 Sept. 2019).
172 Below, Social History; Religious History
173 NHLE, nos 1178575, Park Farmhouse; 1302409, The Church Cottage (accessed 30 Sept. 2019).
174 NHLE, nos 1082125, Bridge Cottage; 1082126, Brook House; 1082161, Fortey Cottage; 1178833, High Gate (accessed 30 Sept. 2019).
175 NHLE, nos 1082159, Barton Cottages; 1178719, Broadleigh; 1302320, Barton Cottages; 1349712, Netherpaths Farmhouse (accessed 30 Sept. 2019).
176 Below, Social History.
177 NHLE, nos 1302265, Barn About 30 yd. SW of Hartlands; 1302297, Hartlands; 1349719, Barn About 15 yd. SW of Hartlands (accessed 30 Sept. 2019); Brooks and Pevsner, *Herefs.* 181.
178 NHLE, no. 1082145, Oldcastle Farmhouse (accessed 30 Sept. 2019).
179 NHLE, no. 1082150, Petty France Farmhouse (accessed 30 Sept. 2019).
180 Below, Landownership.
181 Census, 1851; 1881; 1901.

between Colwall Stone and the Wyche Cutting. These include the Winnings, owned by the prominent local engineer Stephen Ballard, which was constructed after 1852 on the site of an older farmhouse of the same name.[182] It is three bays wide and two storeys high and is heavily classical in detail. Also built in the 1860s by the Ballard family were the Quarry, 'Tudorish' in style with an Italianate lodge dated 1863,[183] and New Court, which was demolished in 1926.

At Colwall Stone, several cottages marked on the tithe map of 1841 had been replaced by modern brick buildings by 1885, such as the Crown inn and the building subsequently occupied as a post office, both on Walwyn Road next to the eponymous Colwall stone, and a row of cottages on Silver Street.[184] By the end of the century the approach to Colwall Stone along Walwyn Road from the north-east was lined by substantial houses and shops, built of brick with stone quoins, and many of them featuring decorative timbers in projecting gables.[185] Two rows of shops, each comprising four bays with large shop fronts in the projecting gables, and featuring date stones from the late 1890s and initials for members of the Pedlingham family, faced modern stone houses. Opposite Stone Farm a single storey bank was also constructed of brick, with V-strut timbers in the gables, and a Welsh slate roof. The Stores, on Walwyn Road south of Colwall Stone, is similarly a double fronted shop built in the late 19th century. Away from Walwyn Road, several large semi-detached houses, also of brick with decorated gables, were laid out along the lanes that would become the Crescent, Crescent Road, and Albert Road.

The Ballard family played a prominent role in the development of Colwall, particularly through the involvement of Stephen Ballard with the construction of the railway line, as well as a number of other industrial enterprises within the village that further stimulated its growth. During the later 19th and early 20th centuries they constructed a number of buildings in the parish, both industrial and residential. Several of these lay along Stone Drive, the lane laid out between Colwall Stone and Old Church Road c.1863.[186] At its southern end, the Temperance Hotel was built in 1880 of concrete using ballast from the Ballards' estate quarry, and the Workmen's Hall was built in 1890. The building later housed a free library, and was demolished in 1974.[187] Opposite, on Stone Drive, is one of Ballard's standard lodges. To the north of these stood the Ballards' vinegar works, opened c.1884 and significantly expanded before 1903.[188] At the northern end of Stone Drive, Grovesend was built by the younger Stephen Ballard in 1894.[189] The former Malvern water bottling plant was designed by Truefitt and Truefitt, and built on Walwyn Road c.1891–2.[190] It was demolished in 2010, apart from the tank house which

182 Brooks and Pevsner, *Herefs.* 179; HAS, L229; OS Map, 25" (1887 edn), Herefordshire XXXVI.6.
183 Brooks and Pevsner, *Herefs.* 179.
184 HAS, L229; OS Map, 25" (1887 edn), Herefordshire XXXVI.6.
185 OS Map, 25" (1905 edn), Herefordshire XXXVI.6.
186 HAS, AA86/2, p. 11.
187 Ballard, *Colwall Collection*, 14; OS Maps, 25" (1905 edn), Herefordshire XXXVI.6; 1:10000 (1974 edn), SO74SW; below, Social History.
188 OS Maps, 25" (1887, 1905 edns.), Herefordshire XXXVI.6; below, Economic History.
189 Brooks and Pevsner, *Herefs.* 178.
190 *The Builder*, 62 (1892), 80; H.A.N. Brockman, *The British Architect in Industry 1841–1940* (1974), 71–2; Brooks and Pevsner, *Herefs.* 178.

replicated the building at the Holy Well in Malvern Wells.[191] It is one and a half storeys high and constructed of brick in a Tudor cottage style. Laboratory Cottage on Silver Street was built by Stephen Ballard to conduct chemical experiments associated with his vinegar works. Further north of Colwall Stone the concrete lodge of Old Court is a standard Ballard construction.

To the south of Colwall Stone, 'Railway Terrace' at the junction of Walwyn Road and Mill Lane was built by 1903.[192] Few new buildings had been erected around Colwall Green by the end of the century, but at its southern end, where Evendine Lane met Walwyn Road, two influential buildings, Bryn Bella House (now two dwellings) and Victoria House, were constructed c.1897. Built largely of red brick, they feature yellow brick dressings on a blue brick plinth, a style adopted by several other cottages in the area. All are late examples of permanent polychrome brickwork.

In 1885 Upper Colwall remained largely a collection of cottages dispersed along the edges of the common land below the ridge of the Malvern Hills, although by that date Knell New House had been constructed to the south of Knell Farm.[193] By the early 20th century a number of new houses and cottages lined the roads of Upper Colwall, particularly close to Wyche Cutting. Several large buildings were built at Upper Colwall by Stephen Ballard in the late 19th century, many in concrete.[194] One of these, Sunfold, is roughcast, has a flat roof with battlements and a round corner turret with a domed roof; shuttered concrete was used for its construction in 1912.[195]

At the base of the Herefordshire Beacon, an 18th-century rendered building was enlarged to become by 1853 the British Camp Hotel.[196] An open-air swimming pool was built on the opposite side of the road, perhaps as part of a redevelopment of the hotel as a road house during the 1930s, but the pool had closed by 1950, and was subsequently filled in.[197] The hotel, now the Malvern Hills Hotel, was enlarged again in 2016–7. Nearby, Wynd's Point is a gabled stone house which is 'rambling and cottagey' in style.[198] It was constructed by William Johnson, a Malvern builder, for himself c.1860. It was purchased in 1883 by the soprano Johanna Maria, known as Jenny Lind, the 'Swedish Nightingale'. It was subsequently purchased by George and Robert Cadbury, of the family of chocolate manufacturers, as a 'place of rest' for themselves, their families and groups of Birmingham workers or children.[199]

Arts and Crafts houses: Perrycroft, Brand Lodge and Black Hill

The construction of Jubilee Drive, running between Wyche Cutting and Wynd's Point below the ridge of the Malvern Hills and affording stunning views across the

191 NHLE, no. 1396465, The Tank House, Coca Cola Enterprises Ltd (accessed 30 Sept. 2019); Smith, *Malvern*, 198.
192 OS Map, 25" (1905 edn), Herefordshire XXXVI.6.
193 HAS, L229; OS Map, 25" (1887 edn), Herefordshire XXXVI.6.
194 P. Hurle, *Stephen Ballard*, 82–3.
195 Ballard, *Colwall Collection*, 14–15, 88–9.
196 Brooks and Pevsner, *Herefs*. 18; below, Social History.
197 *Kelly's Dir. of Herefs.* (1937); (1941), 44; MHC minute books, 1947–54, p. 92; 1954–9, p. 76; 1963–6, pp. 188, 200; 1969–72, p. 38; inf. from Matthew Bristow, 31 Aug. 2018.
198 Brooks and Pevsner, *Herefs*. 181.
199 A.G. Gardiner, *Life of George Cadbury* (1923), 258.

Figure 7 *Drawing of the south elevation of Perrycroft by C.F.A. Voysey produced in 1894.*

area, stimulated the construction of a number of noteworthy houses along its length. Perrycroft, the first large-scale country house commission of the architect Charles Voysey,[200] is an innovative example of an Arts and Crafts house which melds tradition and modernity in a strikingly original way, erected between 1893 and 1895.[201] Facing south with views dominated by British Camp, the house was built for John William Wilson, an MP and industrialist, who subsequently donated other tracts of hill land to the Malvern Hills conservators to prevent further development. The house, altered and enlarged by Voysey in 1907 and again in 1924, is L-shaped and built of brick roughcast painted white. It has a hipped roof covered with green Westmorland slate, and a series of battered chimneys. The entrance front to the north, with a two-storey porch, is 'amazingly un-Victorian, yet not without grandeur.'[202] The service wing to the north-east has a half-timbered water tower, fed with Malvern spring water and topped with a flat ogee lead roof and a tall weather cock.[203] By contrast the broader, partially jettied, southern front is 'unpretentious, sensible and graceful',[204] with corner buttresses and a recessed ground floor centre. The external woodwork is painted a distinct shade of green specified by Voysey,[205] and two chimney pieces and a fireplace are faced with green Connemara marble. Voysey also prepared plans for the walled garden, laid out in 1895, and the pyramid-roofed summer house constructed in 1904.[206] The ancillary buildings include two sets of stables, dated 1903, an L-shaped coach house with its accompanying

200 P. Davey, *Arts and Crafts Architecture* (New York, 1980), 88; *ODNB*, s.v. Voysey, Charles Francis Annesley, architect and designer (accessed 30 Sept. 2019).
201 Brooks and Pevsner, *Herefs.* 180–1; NHLE, no. 1178660, Perrycroft (accessed 30 Sept. 2019); HER, 6711, 31188; *Country Life*, 205: 29 (2011), 72–5.
202 Brooks and Pevsner, *Herefs.* 180–1.
203 RIBA, 69266.
204 Brooks and Pevsner, *Herefs.* 180.
205 RIBA, 69267, 94265.
206 NHLE, no. 1349715, Summerhouse, Gate, Boundary Walls *c.*60 yd. SW of Perrycroft with associated walls (accessed 30 Sept. 2019).

Figure 8 *Photograph of the exterior of Perrycroft in 1894.*

cottage, and the coachman's cottage, built in 1908, and the T-shaped gate lodge built in 1914.[207]

South of Perrycroft, Brand Lodge is another fine Arts and Crafts house, built for Julia Holland to designs by Ernest Newton in 1910–11 on the site of an 18th-century house of the same name.[208] It is roughcast with a roof of Westmorland slate, and faces west with a semi-circular Ionic porch at its centre. The gabled wings have shallow lead-faced polygonal bay windows of two storeys. It has a simpler entrance front to the east, with a central two-storey porch crowned by a broken-curved pediment. To the north-east is a large service wing. By the road are the former stables and power house, later extended, which follow a U-shaped plan. At the southern end of Jubilee Drive near British Camp is Black Hill, one of the last Arts and Crafts houses to be built in Britain.[209] It has been suggested that the house built in 1917 for Sir Barry Vincent Jackson was designed by William de Lacy Aherne, who was responsible for numerous houses in the Moseley area of Birmingham.[210]

20th–Century Buildings

A group of buildings were erected by Roland Cave-Brown-Cave early in the 20th century to complement his new racecourse.[211] Echoing the extant timber-framed buildings such as Stone Holt, and the timbered gables of shop fronts erected in the 1890s, Cave-Brown-Cave's group were built in a mock-Tudor style, of red brick and decorative black-and-

207 NHLE, nos 1082156, Perrycroft Lodge; 1178680, Stables *c.*75 yd. NW of Perrycroft Lodge (accessed 30 Sept. 2019).
208 Brooks and Pevsner, *Herefs.* 181; NHLE, no. 1349714, Brand Lodge (accessed 30 Sept. 2019).
209 Brooks and Pevsner, *Herefs.* 181. *ODNB*, s.v. Jackson, Sir Barry Vincent, theatre director (accessed 30 Sept. 2019); below, Social History.
210 C. Wood, 'William de Lacy Aherene', in P. Ballard, *Birmingham's Victorian and Edwardian Architects* (Wetherby, 2009), 578–83.
211 Below, Social History.

white timbering. The most substantial of these, and perhaps the most striking building in the centre of Colwall Stone, Colwall Park Hotel was built in 1903 immediately to the west of the station, to plans by H. Percy Smith of Worcester. The ground floor is brick with mullioned and transomed windows, the upper storey is half-timbered with wooden gables and oriels. Three-storey gables project from both wings of the building, of two bays to the left and one wide bay to the right, the top level jettied, as is the gable of the two-storey central porch. A planned clocktower was not built.[212] In a similar if less substantial style is the Horse and Jockey public house and stables. At the south-east corner of Colwall Green are the former racecourse stables.[213] Originally intended to form a V-shaped building at the corner of Evendine Lane and Cave's Folly, only the two-storey entrance block and the single-storey south range of the stables were completed. Built of rubble with brick dressings and hung with tiles on the upper level, the main block contains the arched entrance to the courtyard, now blocked in, over which projects a half-timbered gable.

A small number of semi-detached estate cottages were built at Colwall Green in the years after 1913 designed by Arthur Troyte Griffith of Malvern, a friend of Sir Edward Elgar. He also designed the plain brick Fox Court built at the end of Lower Ballard Drive in 1931.[214] Along the West Malvern Road is the former Royal Wells Brewery, five storeys high and two bays wide, dated 1905. Nearby are earlier villa-like buildings, including Royal Spa Lodge with pilasters and foliated capitals, and Victoria Cottage with carved stone details in its porch. A wrought-iron shelter with a tiled roof at the top of Upper Colwall was erected in memory of Lt. Col. A. H. Boulton, who died in the First World War.[215] The large single-storey red-brick village hall in Mill Lane opened in 1992.[216] Opposite Sunfold is Lobden, a rare example of an early modernist house, built in 1932 by R. D. Russell with Marian Pepler. Originally rendered white, it has flat roofs and was extended in 1955.[217] A square clock tower in Walwyn Road, of Malvern Stone with ashlar dressings and a flat concrete roof, was built in 1931 for Thomas Alfred Pedlingham as a memorial to his wife Alice and is known locally as Aunt Alice.[218] Behind it is the library, begun in 1955 to a design by Alexander Graham; a meeting room was added in 2002.[219]

212 Brooks and Pevsner, *Herefs*. 178; a presentation drawing is displayed in the hotel.
213 Brooks and Pevsner, *Herefs*. 178; NHLE, no. 1082164, Upper House and Attached Former Stable (accessed 30 Sept. 2019).
214 J.M. Hardie, *Troyte Griffith: Malvern Architect and Elgar's Friend* (2012); Brooks and Pevsner, *Herefs*. 179.
215 NHLE, no. 1082124, Shelter and Belvedere at NGR SO768436 (accessed 30 Sept. 2019).
216 *Colwall Clock,* Dec. 1994; below, Social History.
217 WAAS, 705:876 BA8077 90ii; Brooks and Pevsner, *Herefs*. 179.
218 WAAS, 705.876 BA 8077 21; Brooks and Pevsner, *Herefs*. 178.
219 Below, Social History, Local Government.

THE BRITISH CAMP

BRITISH CAMP, A SUBSTANTIAL EARTHWORK enclosure encircling the Herefordshire Beacon, lies mostly in Colwall parish, but extends into the parishes of Ledbury Rural and Little Malvern.[1] At a height of 338 m., the British Camp summit is the highest point on the ridge of the Malvern Hills within Herefordshire. The name Herefordshire Beacon was recorded in 1628,[2] and imitates its northern neighbour in Worcestershire, at 425 m. the highest summit of the Malvern Hills, and both hills were used as fire-beacons at times of alarm or celebration.[3] During the Civil War the high constable of Radlow Hundred was required to maintain the fire signal on Herefordshire Beacon.[4] A large platform at the summit may indicate levelling to form a plinth.

The massive earthwork entrenchments of British Camp were mostly constructed in the 1st millennium BC, while the upstanding central works on the summit were created as part of a medieval ring-work castle placed centrally within the prehistoric enclosure. This castle, the summit part of which is known also as the Citadel, probably originated in the late 11th century. A circuit of prehistoric banks and ditches slightly lower down the summit were adapted to create the bailey. It seems likely that a stone component was soon added and ceramic evidence suggests that the main period of use was from the mid 12th century to mid 13th century.

Treadway Nash was the first to argue, in 1799, that the camp was not Roman, as had previously been believed, and in 1822 Revd Henry Card, vicar of Great Malvern, argued that the camp was constructed by the ancient Briton Caractacus.[5] By 1856 the inn at the foot of the hill was known as the British Camp inn, the name presumably intended to lure visitors,[6] and a decade later the landlord of the inn promoted the idea that the Malvern Hills were one of the strongholds of the ancient Britons in their struggle against the Romans.[7] Similar antiquarian accounts published by the Advertiser Office, Malvern brought the legend to local prominence.[8] In 1897, following a visit to Colwall, the mother of Edward Elgar suggested that he compose a tale about the hillfort, resulting in the cantata *Caractacus*, the first scene of which is set in the Malvern Hills.[9] The prominence

---

1   Above, Colwall Parish.

2   Society of Antiquaries of London, MS 520/VI/5 68.2.

3   Smith, *Malvern*, 15.

4   D. Ross, *Royalist but … Herefs. in the English civil war 1640–51* (Almeley, 2012), 9; J. Webb, *Memorials of the civil war between King Charles I and the Parliament of England as it affected Herefs. and the Adjacent Counties* (1879), I, 71.

5   T.R. Nash, *Collections for a History of Worcs.* (1799), 142; H. Card, *A Dissertation on the Subject of Herefs. Beacon* (1822).

6   *PO Dir.* (1856 edn).

7   P. Pockett, *An Account of the Herefs. Beacon* (Malvern, 1867); *Heref. Times*, 13 July 1867.

8   J. McKay, *The British Camp on the Herefs. Beacon: Fifteen Short Essays* (Malvern, 1875).

9   J.N. Moore, *Edward Elgar: A Creative Life* (Oxford, 1984), 225.

Figure 9 *Photograph of the earthworks on British Camp.*

of this piece, and the proximity of the eponymous hotel, appear to have permanently fixed the name British Camp, once a term used commonly to refer to any hillfort thought to have been constructed by the ancient Britons, but which in many places has fallen out of use since the 19th century.

The Origins of British Camp

Although the Shire Ditch was employed during the Middle Ages as a boundary to divide the bishop of Hereford's chase from Malvern Chase, and Herefordshire from Worcestershire, it is thought to have originated in the Middle Bronze Age (*c.*1500–800BC).[10] If the ditch, which extends across the eastern flank of the British Camp, predates the hillfort, it may have served as an early boundary marker. An oval-shaped enclosure, largely obliterated by the construction of the medieval ring-work, perhaps dates from early in the 1st millennium BC, and may have been constructed with or shortly after the ditch.

A single ring of massive banks and ditches encircles the hilltop below the summit, forming an egg-shaped enclosure aligned east–west that encloses *c.*½ ha. and marks a second phase of development. Only the north-eastern and eastern sides of these earthworks survive largely intact, the rest having been subsumed by later developments. The interior of this early hillfort is mostly occupied by the Norman ring-work, but at least a dozen crescentic or semi-circular platforms survive on its east-facing slopes. A possible original entrance to the enclosure faced north-eastwards down the natural ridge-spur that extends towards Wynds Gap.

British Camp: a Developed Hillfort

The construction of the developed hillfort called the British Camp marks a third phase of development. At its maximum extent it is one of the largest works ever created in Iron

10   M. Bowden, *The Malvern Hills: a Sacred Landscape* (Swindon, 2005), 16–7.

Figure 10 *Photograph of the earthworks on British Camp, looking north towards the Wyche and Worcestershire Beacon.*

Age Britain.[11] This explains its visual prominence, and is also a testament to the labour invested in its construction on the hard pre-Cambrian rocks of the ridge-top. This huge scale is matched by the complexity of the edifice, which closely follows the topography along the *c*.3 km extent of the earthworks. The impressive height of the banks results from extensive scarping back of the natural slopes above ditches some distance down the hillside, which were dug in part to create a counterscarp bank on their outer lip. The camp ranges along the summit of the hill, extending over 900 m. The defences alone occupy over 6 ha., and the area enclosed must be somewhere in the region of 10 ha. The four entrances through these ramparts appear to have been deliberately planned and built.

The main features include the earlier circuit that was abandoned on its north-eastern side to extend the hillfort some 250 m. north-eastwards to dramatically overlook Wynds Gap. This involved a descent of 60 m. down a steep gradient onto the northern spur of the ridge, where a series of massive quarry pits was dug. Within this narrow 1 ha. area, enclosed by a relatively small-scale rampart which may have been surmounted by a timber and stone wall or palisade, at least 30 platforms appear to indicate the existence of a number of buildings and yards, although some of these may have been of medieval or modern origin. To the east of the northern extremity of the ramparts there appears to have been an east-facing gateway.

The slightly longer south-facing spur of the camp comprises a rocky spine rising to a craggy summit that is both denuded but also apparently devoid of substantial early features. There are more building platforms located on the north-facing slope, but none have been recorded on the gently sloping south-facing side. Another east-facing entrance, close to the southern tip of the camp, appears to mirror that at the northern

11   M. Bowden, *British Camp or Herefs. Beacon*, English Heritage Archaeological Investigations Report AI/124/2000; Bowden, *Malvern Hills*, 19–22.

end. Two more entrances were positioned diagonally opposite each other immediately below the Citadel, at the narrowest part of the camp, where the ramparts which form the northern end of the southern spur are 35 m. apart. The western entrance, the better preserved, is approached diagonally up the scarp of the hill from the south-west, crossing the main west-facing ditch of the hillfort on a causeway. It appears the gate passage was deliberately angled, and inside the gate structure a level area is bounded on either side by quarry ditches behind the bank. The gateway area itself is overlooked from the east by a series of scarped platforms.

The most complex area of the developed hillfort is the arc of steeply sloping ground that makes up its eastern side, beneath which lies a reservoir constructed in the 19th century to serve Great Malvern. The complexity is due to the extensive terracing of the hillside here, above the outer hillfort rampart, and arises also from the fact that at some point there was a significant alteration of the plan, probably to modify an original entrance and to enclose more ground. The original course of the main hillfort bank, the vestiges of which remain traceable, gently curved to the north before turning abruptly eastwards, forming a steep south-facing scarp beneath the outer rampart. A track passed through a simple entrance through the bank and descended eastwards. The alteration involved turning the bank abruptly to the eastwards further to the south, causing it to travel sharply downslope before continuing north-eastwards to re-join the main bank and scarp around the northern spur. A short length of upstanding bank was inserted within the main bank to create a new double gateway.

The Norman Ring-Work

A ring-work is an earthwork that comprises a broadly circular or oval bank with a central enclosed area and standing prominently above a deep encircling ditch. The earthen ring-work at Herefordshire Beacon is unique in the county in that it survives as first built, and the character of the ring-work bank puts it into a rare class nationally.

The ovoid ring-work of the Citadel is broader to the west and narrows slightly eastwards. It comprises a conical mound surmounted by a low encircling bank that is more prominent on the eastern side. Inside the bank the ground tilts eastwards and there are several variations in ground-level that may correlate both with the location of former buildings and with Hilton Price's excavation trenches dug in 1879.[12] Its exterior comprises a steep scarp descending into a deep rock-cut ditch some 8–10 m. below the bank. Rock dug from this ditch was probably used to heighten the mound and may also have been used to create a level counterscarp platform edged to the east by a low bank. This external platform has been described as a 'micro-bailey'. However, it seems more likely that the area to the east of the ring-work but still on the summit contains the remnant of an elongated late-prehistoric summit-top enclosure that was partially covered with rock and soil from the ring-work ditch.

The land upon which the castle was built was the bishop of Hereford's, and the castle was in existence by 1148, when the earl of Gloucester was in possession of this part of the Malvern Hills.[13] It has been suggested that the castle was besieged and possibly changed

12   F. G. Hilton Price, 'Camps', 217–28.
13   P. Remfry, *The Herefs. Beacon and the families of King Harold II and the earls of Heref. and Worc.* (Malvern, 2008), pp. 26–7, 34–5.

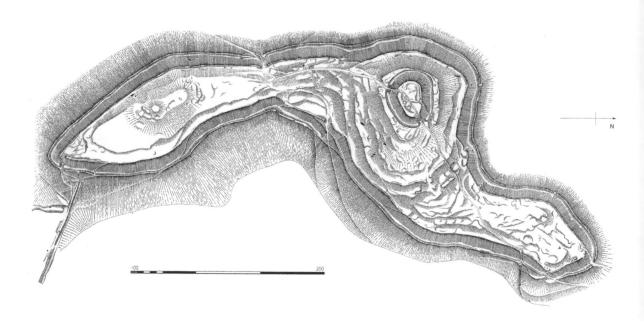

Figure 11 *Measured Survey of British Camp and Herefordshire Beacon.*

hands several times in the early 1150s towards the end of Stephen's reign, before being destroyed by Henry II in 1155.[14] However, the reliability of the records of these events is uncertain.

In the 19th century the Herefordshire Beacon attracted the attention of several archaeologists including Gen. Pitt-Rivers.[15] H. H. Lines, a landscape artist with an interest in archaeology, investigated the earthworks in 1869 producing archaeological drawings and a landscape painting of British Camp.[16] The only documented archaeological excavation is Hilton Price's work of 1879, who dug five trenches within the Citadel.[17] These produced mainly medieval finds, including an arrow-head, a metal spur, and a large quantity of animal bones and deer antler, suggesting that the remote site may primarily have served as a hunting lodge.[18]

Exactly what form the buildings sited on the bleak hilltop might have taken is uncertain, but the masses of charcoal recorded in the excavations of 1879 may indicate that timber made up part of structures that also included clay-bonded rubble stone walls. A platform within the upper western part of the Citadel could have served as a small motte, or at least have provided the base for a principal tower, and there were clearly structures built against the inside of the rampart on the eastern side.

14   Remfry, The Herefs. Beacon p.34-5.
15   *VCH Herefs.* I, 205–6.
16   *Worc. Jnl,* 1 May 1869. The drawings are held by Worc. City Art Gallery.
17   Hilton Price, 'Camps', 221–2; *Worcs. Ceramics Online Database,* https://worcestershireceramics.org/fabrics/3 and /48 (accessed 11 May 2019).
18   R. Higham and P. Barker, *Timber Castles* (Exeter, 1992), 200, 239.

The suggestion that a causeway crossing the ditch on the southern flank of the summit represents the original gateway into the Citadel is difficult to substantiate given the extent of visitor erosion and modern conservation works. A more plausible entrance would be via a bridge or causeway through the gap in the north-eastern part of the bank circuit. This would broadly align with the entrance-gap through the early circuit of substantial Iron Age defences lower down the north-east facing spur. This entrance has been interpreted as forming an out-turned prehistoric gateway, but it could also be a Norman or 12th-century modification of an early entrance, with the out-turned slight horn-work banks serving as a crude barbican.

Later Developments

At the northern perimeter of the Beacon is a crescent shaped earthwork with a slight depression above it with a box mound behind. These are thought to be a gun emplacement and slit trench positioned during the Second World War to overlook the road climbing up to Wynds Point from the east.[19] The Home Guard were trained in the use of 6-pdr anti-tank guns near the reservoir.[20]

19   Bowden, *Malvern Hills*, 51; HER, 30519.
20   A. Simons, *British Camp* (Malvern, 2011), 57.

LANDOWNERSHIP

Pattern of Landownership

THE MANOR OF COLWALL BELONGED to the bishops of Hereford from at least the 11th century, and probably earlier, until 1868. A sizeable estate in the south of the parish was taken from the bishop's manor to endow the prebend of Barton Colwall in the 11th or 12th century. Another estate, taking its name from the Brockbury family that held it in the 13th and 14th centuries, was reputed a manor by the 16th century. From the 16th century onwards gentry families built up sizeable estates in the parish, including Hope End, Old Colwall, and the Hoar.

Manors and Principal Estates

Colwall Manor

Colwall was among a block of estates near the Malvern Hills held by the bishop of Hereford by the 11th century, which were probably originally granted to the see by Mildfrith, king of the Magonsaete, in the late 7th century.[1] Following the sack of Hereford cathedral in 1055 and the vacancy of the see in 1056, Harold Godwinson took possession of Colwall with other episcopal estates, in his capacity as earl of Hereford. The manor was restored to the bishop following the Norman Conquest.[2] It was confiscated with all other episcopal estates in 1322, and between 1324 and 1327, for Bishop Orleton's rebellion against Edward II, but subsequently restored.[3] Under the terms of the Act of 1860, the manor was vested in the Ecclesiastical Commissioners after the death of Bishop Hampden in 1868.[4]

If there was a manor house at Colwall in the 14th century, it was not one of those it was decided in 1356 should be kept in good repair.[5] The bishop had a park at Colwall by 1262,[6] and Park Farm, north-west of the parish church, is said to stand on the site of the bishop's lodge.[7] The timber-framed house, comprising three parallel ranges each of five bays and two storeys, was built in two phases during the 16th century. The larger

1 *Fasti Eccles. Ang. 1066–1300, VIII, xxi–xxv.*
2 *Domesday*, 502.
3 *Cal. Pat.* 1321–4, 452; *Cal. Fine R.* 1319–27, 307; *VCH Herefs. Bosbury*, 22.
4 23 & 24 Vic. c.124; LPL, ECE/6/1/54; ECE/7/1/26738; ECE/7/1/77153; *Fasti Eccles. Ang. 1541–1857*, XIII, 10–11.
5 *Charters and Records of Heref. Cathedral*, ed. W.W. Capes (Heref. 1908), 226–9.
6 *Cal. Pat.* 1258–66, 232; below, Economic History.
7 J.W. Tonkin, 'The palaces of the bishop of Hereford', *TWNFC*, 124 (1976), 54; D. Whitehead, 'Some connected thoughts on the parks and gardens of Herefs. before the age of landscape gardening', *TWNFC* (1995), 205; HAS, AA59/A/2, f. 68.

Figure 12 *Photograph of Park Farm in 1929.*

north wing may have been an addition to an earlier hall, which was demolished later in the century to make way for the central and south wings.[8] The three ranges are gabled at both the east and west ends, faced with wattle and daub between close-set studs, and each range topped with a roof of tile. The south front is faced in brick and has a substantial external chimney stack. There is one original timber oriel on the north front, and shallow bay windows on the north and west fronts. North of the farmhouse is an extensive range of brick farm buildings erected by T. Nicholson in 1867, now converted to residential use. Park Farm was sold to the Ballard family in 1910. Badly dilapidated, the house was purchased by the Duddy family in 2001, who began to restore it in 2004.[9]

Barton Colwall

Land at the bishop's barton in Colwall, amounting to two ploughlands, were taken in the late 11th or early 12th century to endow a prebend in Hereford cathedral.[10] The names of prebendaries are recorded from 1268, when John Walraund was appointed by the king during an episcopal vacancy.[11] In 1279 the prebendary was granted free warren in his demesne at the Barton in Colwall and Hope, presumably Hope End.[12] In 1291 the prebendary held two carucates of land, valued at £6 13s. 4d., and rents amounted to another £6 13s. 4d.[13] An early-15th-century dispute between the prebendary John

8   NHLE, no. 1178575, Park Farmhouse (accessed 30 Sept. 2019); RCHME, *Inventory*, II, 52–7; A. Bouchier and R.K. Morriss, Park Farm Preliminary Analysis (2004), report held in HER.

9   *Colwall Clock*, Sept. 2005.

10 *Fasti Eccles. Ang. 1066–1300*, VIII, xxiv–xxv.

11 *Cal. Pat.* 1266–72, 306; *Fasti Eccles. Ang. 1066–1300*, VIII, 33–4; 1300–1541, II, 18–9; 1541–1857, XIII, 39–41.

12 *Cal. Pat.* 1272–81, 302.

13 *Tax. Eccles.* (Rec. Com.), 169.

Bridbroke and Malcolm Walwyn may have concerned the manor's boundaries with his estate at Massington.[14]

From at least the 16th century the manor was farmed to tenants. Charles Trovell and his brother-in-law John Skinner held their first court as lords in 1587.[15] A new lease for three lives was granted to Trovell and his son-in-law Giles Nanfan in 1607.[16] In 1687 the manor house and demesne lands were let to Robert Wylde of Worcester for 21 years,[17] and it was held by tenants during the 18th and early 19th centuries.[18] Following a lengthy suit in Chancery concerning the will of Henry Lambert, the tenant from 1789 until his death in 1814,[19] the estate passed to his great-grandson Reynolds Peyton.[20] The reversion of the manor was vested in the Ecclesiastical Commissioners by the Act of 1840,[21] who sold their interest to Peyton in 1851.[22] He died in 1861,[23] and the estate passed to his mother (d. 1862), and then to his brother Thomas Griffith Peyton,[24] who took possession of the manor on the death of the last prebendary in 1867.[25] His brother Nicholson Julius Peyton succeeded to the estate in 1887.[26] He sold the manorial rights to Robert Raper of Hoe Court c.1905,[27] who remained the lord at his death in 1915,[28] although he had transferred his rights over the Herefordshire Beacon to the Malvern Hills conservators c.1905.[29]

The remainder of the estate, including Barton Court, was sold c.1881–5 to Benjamin Bright, son of Benjamin Heywood Bright (d. 1843),[30] who had inherited the majority of the property of Henry Bright of Brockbury in 1869.[31] Following Benjamin Bright's death in 1900, the estate passed to his daughter Honora, wife of Roland Cave-Brown-Cave.[32] The estate was put up for sale in 1905, when it comprised 1,636 a. and included ten farms, the Horse & Groom inn, and Colwall Park racecourse.[33] The Cave-Brown-Caves were still in possession in 1906, when they sought to obtain a mortgage of £50,000 on the estate,[34] and it was put up for sale again in 1913, 1915, and 1919.[35] It was purchased

14 TNA, C 1/6/145.
15 HAS, AE30/435.
16 HAS, AA26/II/43.
17 HAS, AA26/II/45–6, 50.
18 HAS, AA26/II/53–4, 56, 59, 62–3, 67–70.
19 TNA, PROB 11/1557/455.
20 TNA, C 13/1769/34; C 13/1789/34; C 101/2840; *English Reports Full Reprint*, XXXVIII (Chancery, XVIII), 971–80; *Russell*, V, 116–42; *Barnewall and Cresswell*, VI, 403–22.
21 3 & 4 Vic. c.113.
22 LPL, ECE/6/1/53, pp. 291, 299–300; ECE/7/1/351–2.
23 HAS, AA26/I/2.
24 HAS, AA26/I/2; AA26/II/71–4.
25 *Fasti Eccles. Ang.* 1541–1857, XIII, 41.
26 *National Probate Calendar*, Wills, 1887.
27 HAS, AA26/II/76–8; AA26/IV/3, 6.
28 Below, Hoe Court.
29 Below, Local Government.
30 *Herald & Genealogist*, VII (1873), 505; *Burke's Family Records* (1897), 97.
31 *National Probate Calendar*, Wills, 1869.
32 MHC, Abstract of title to Barton Court.
33 Historic England Archives, SC00449; *The Times*, 1 July 1905.
34 GA, D2299/1/1/675.
35 HAS, AO12/18/15; M5/6/62–4; GA, D4858/2/3/1913/2; Historic England Archives, SC00450; Malvern Library L33.335; *The Times*, 21 June 1913; 30 Aug. 1919.

Figure 13 *Photograph of Dovecote at Barton Court.*

privately in 1920 by the Liverpool merchant Allan Heywood Bright,[36] the great-nephew of Benjamin Bright (d. 1900).[37] He died in 1941,[38] and his widow Kelbourn Milroy Bright died in 1961, when the estate, then comprising *c*.397 a., passed to their daughter Elizabeth Mary Lloyd, wife of Michael Charles Fox Lloyd.[39] It was purchased in 2015 by James and Linda Meyer, the present owners.[40]

Barton Court was largely rebuilt for Henry Lambert. Fronted in red brick with a hipped roof, the wide third bay, topped with a pediment, renders the six-bay house asymmetrical. In the pediment is a half-moon window, above a Venetian window on the first floor, and a porch of the 1820s, perhaps the original entrance reused. The ground floor is dominated by the three-bay dining room in the south-east corner, decorated in a Robert Adam style. The house was extended to the north-east *c*.1895 with a single-storey range fronted by a canted bay at the junction. Weatherboarding to the rear of the house dates from the early 18th century.[41]

Behind the house are several farm buildings. The long 17th-century barn, with two threshing floors, was probably originally of six bays, but the north end was truncated

36   *Cheltenham Chron.* 20 Sept. 1919.
37   *Herald & Genealogist*, VII (1873), 503–11.
38   *The Times*, 5 Aug. 1941; *London Gaz.* 14 Oct. 1941, p. 6001.
39   MHC, Abstract of title of E.M. Lloyd to land at Colwall.
40   *Barton Court*, https://www.bartoncourtonline.co.uk (accessed 13 May 2019); pers. inf.
41   Brooks and Pevsner, *Herefs.* 177; NHLE, no. 1082152, Barton Court (accessed 30 Sept. 2019).

when stables were built in the 19th century.[42] The circular rubble dovecote may be late-medieval in origin.[43]

Brockbury

There is no evidence to support the suggestion that there was a cell of Great Malvern priory at Brockbury.[44]

Philip Ruddock (d. bef. 1270) held four yardlands (*virgates*) as a sixth of a knight's fee in Colwall in the middle of the 13th century, the basis of the later manor.[45] By the late 13th century this had passed to William of *Brocbury*, whose family took their name from their manor in the parish of Brobury,[46] and which name was subsequently attached to their Colwall estate. In 1314 he or a namesake held a messuage, 160 a. of land, 11 a. of meadow, 2 a. of pasture, and 5 a. of wood in Colwall and Coddington.[47] William, still living in 1323,[48] had been succeeded by his son James by 1348,[49] who died between 1365 and 1372.[50] The estate was held by Robert of Prestbury and his wife Margery in 1377, when they granted it to John of Blakeney and his wife Agnes.[51] By the early 15th century the estate had passed to Thomas Cowley, who died in 1437 or 1438.[52] William Cowley of Colwall did homage for four yardlands of free land held by one-sixth part of a knight's fee in 1455,[53] and in 1546 a namesake held the estate, then described as a manor and comprising *c.*400 a. of land in Colwall and Coddington.[54] His heir was his son Thomas Cowley who sold the estate *c.*1566 to John Walwyn.[55]

John Walwyn made a settlement of the estate in 1571, augmented by land formerly belonging to Little Malvern priory,[56] and it descended to his son Robert in 1587,[57] who in 1610 sold the estate to Henry Bright, prebendary of Pratum Minus.[58] He died in 1627,[59] and in 1631 his widow Joyce and her new husband Edmund Ansley demised her life interest in the estate to trustees, from whom it passed in 1638 to Henry's son Robert.[60] Robert (d. 1665) was succeeded in turn by his son Robert (d. after 1687),[61] and grandson

42   J.E.C. Peters, unpubl. report on Colwall farm buildings; NHLE, no. 1178622, Stable c.55 yd NW of
     Barton Court (accessed 30 Sept. 2019).
43   HER, 3837; NHLE, no. 1178618, Dovecote c.50 yd W of Barton Court (accessed 30 Sept. 2019).
44   Dugdale, *Mon.* III, 447; Smith, *Malvern*, 59.
45   DCA 1079; 1113B–C; HAS, AA59/A/1, f. 160.
46   HAS, AA26/II/10; TNA, CP 25/1/82/31 (81).
47   TNA, CP 25/1/82/31 (81).
48   HAS, AA26/II/11–12, 14.
49   TNA, CP 25/1/82/42 (145).
50   HAS, AA26/II/13, 23, 32.
51   TNA, CP 25/1/83/47 (264).
52   HAS, AA59/A/2, f. 63.
53   *Reg. Stanbury*, 20.
54   HAS, AE30/361.
55   HAS, AE30/54, 345; G87/11/7–9; below, Priory of Great Malvern.
56   HAS, AE30/346–7; below, Priory of Little Malvern.
57   TNA, PROB 11/70/463; HAS, AE30/348.
58   HAS, AE30/350; Fasti Eccles. Ang. 1541–1857, XIII, 103; *Alumni Oxon.* 1500–1714, I, 182.
59   *Fasti Eccles. Ang.* 1541–1857, VII, 123.
60   HAS, AE30/352; *Burke's Landed Gentry* (1937 edn), 235–7.
61   HAS, AE30/354–7.

Figure 14 *Aerial photograph of Brockbury Hall in 1921.*

Robert (d. 1749),[62] who was succeeded in turn by his grandson, also Robert (d. 1758).[63] His son Lowbridge Bright, a merchant at Bristol, was in possession of the estate by 1786.[64] By his will of 1818 the estate was devised to his cousin, Richard Bright of Ham Green (Som.), who died in 1840,[65] and Richard's son Henry, who died in 1869.[66] By Henry's will, the manor passed to his nephew James Franck Bright, son of Dr Richard Bright (d. 1858), and for much of its subsequent history the house was occupied by tenants. Following the death of James Franck Bright in 1920,[67] the Brockbury estate passed to his cousin Allan Heywood Bright who purchased the Barton Court estate in that year. Bright's widow, Kelburn Milroy Bright, was described as lady of the manor at her death in 1961.[68]

62   HAS, AE30/359–60.
63   HAS, AE30/65, 362–3.
64   HAS, AE/30/8; AA26/III/1.
65   TNA, PROB 11/1609/59; PROB 11/1928/309.
66   *National Probate Calendar*, Wills, 1869.
67   *The Times*, 10 Feb. 1921.
68   *Birmingham Daily Post*, 6 Nov. 1961.

Brockbury Hall was built for the Bright family in the late 17th or early 18th century on or near the site of an earlier house, and refaced in red brick later in the century.[69] It is a substantial house, rectangular in plan, comprising six bays by four, on two storeys, with a hipped tile roof. Several of the windows are blocked. Inside the house, one room has 17th-century panelling, and there is a late-17th-century staircase. The rear of the house was refaced in brick in the 20th century.

A plan of Brockbury estate of 1758 shows the house and farm buildings contained within a walled garden, surrounded by landscaped grounds.[70] The possible remains of a moat survive in an orchard north-east of the house. The plan depicts a substantial set of timber-framed farm buildings near the house, perhaps dating from the 17th century, including a dovecote, and a three-bay timber-framed barn with a single threshing floor, none of which survive.[71] An 18th-century bakehouse to the rear of the house incorporates part of a late-medieval cruck truss.[72]

Other Estates

Hope End

Hope End, which takes its name from a hope or valley, lay within the prebendal manor of Barton Colwall,[73] and c.1300 at least two Colwall men were described as 'of Hope'.[74] Thomas Holder of Hope End occurs in 1577;[75] William Holder of Hope End in 1598;[76] John Wheeler of Hope End in 1678;[77] and Richard Gilding of Hope End in 1686.[78] By the 18th century, Hope End was the centre of an estate in Barton Colwall extending into Wellington Heath in Ledbury parish, held by the Pritchard family, first Basil (d. 1749), one of the wealthiest men in the parish,[79] and then his son George (d. 1765).[80] The estate passed to George's daughter Jane (d. 1767),[81] wife of Henry Lambert of Barton Colwall, and then to their daughter Susannah Pritchard,[82] who married Sir Henry Tempest Bt. of Tong (Yorks.).[83] He sold Hope End in 1809 to the Jamaican sugar planter Edward Moulton Barrett, father of the poet Elizabeth Barrett Browning.[84] Barrett sold Hope End c.1832 to the antiquary Thomas Heywood, whose daughter Mary, founder of the

69   Brooks and Pevsner, *Herefs.* 178; NHLE, no. 1349730, Brockbury Hall (accessed 30 Sept. 2019).
70   HAS, AT51; MF General X165; HER, 31679.
71   J.E.C. Peters, unpubl. report on Colwall farm buildings.
72   Brooks and Pevsner, *Herefs.* 178; NHLE, no. 1082184, Detached Bakehouse immediately NW of Brockbury Hall (accessed 30 Sept. 2019).
73   *Cal. Pat.* 1272–81, 302
74   HAS, AA26/II/4, 5, 17.
75   HAS, AA59/A2, f. 69.
76   HAS, 9/3/77, will of John Brooke, 1598.
77   HAS, X2/5/15, will of John Wheeler 1678.
78   HAS, 94/1/30, will of Richard Pitt 1686.
79   HAS, AE30/422; TNA, PROB 11/771/83.
80   HAS, AA26/II/58; B38/184–5; TNA, PROB 11/913/373.
81   *VCH Glos.* XII, 144, 148.
82   TNA, C 101/192.
83   HAS, AA26/II/57–8.
84   NHLE, no. 1000276, Hope End (accessed 30 Sept. 2019).

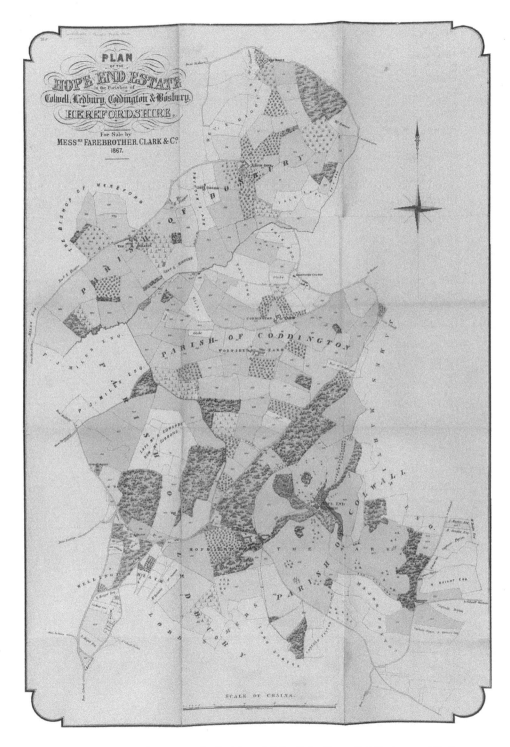

Figure 15 *Plan of the Hope End Estate, in the Parishes of Colwall, Ledbury, Coddington, and Bosbury, Herefordshire, for sale in 1867.*

Figure 16 *Hope End House.*

Mothers' Union, was born there.[85] He died in 1866 and was succeeded by a namesake,[86] who sold the estate *c.*1869 to James Charles Archibald Hewitt.[87] He was succeeded in 1910 by his son John Wilfred Hewitt.[88] The property was sold in 1947 to Stephen Ballard II, and was offered for sale in 1994.[89]

Hope End was erected *c.*1750, probably on or near the site of an older house. In 1796 it was described as a 'partly modern structure, rather large and commodious' with some 'highly finished' apartments.[90] An engraving of 1796 depicts a substantial rectangular three-storey house, of seven bays by three, set within a steep deer park.[91] This house was rebuilt *c.*1810–15 to designs by J. C. Loudon in a Moorish style, with minarets at the

85   *ODNB*, s.v. Heywood, Thomas, antiquary (accessed 30 Sept. 2019); Sumner, Mary, founder of the Mothers' Union (accessed 30 Sept. 2019).
86   *National Probate Calendar*, Wills, 1866; HAS, AA26/I/2.
87   HAS, AA26/I/3, pp. 4–8. *Worc. Jnl,* 5 June 1869.
88   *National Probate Calendar*, Wills, 1910.
89   NHLE, no. 1000276, Hope End (accessed 30 Sept. 2019); CVS newsletter forthcoming; HAS, B472/2.
90   J. Barrett, *A Description of Malvern, and its Environs* (Worc. 1796), 81; Brooks and Pevsner, *Herefs.* 647; NHLE, no. 1082142, Hope End Hotel (accessed 30 Sept. 2019).
91   J. Bluck, *The Seat of Sir H. Tempest* (1796).

eastern end.[92] The house was demolished in 1873 by James Hewitt,[93] who built a large stone mansion in a Gothic style 250 m. to the north, much of which was destroyed by fire in 1910, only the service wing surviving the blaze.[94] Of Loudon's house, all that survives are a gateway and boundary wall with minarets.[95]

The house is set at the centre of a park that was probably laid out in the mid 18th century, and a map of 1754 depicts the house (perhaps fancifully) within a pale.[96] Possibly at the same time fishponds, mentioned in 1765, were formed by damning the Cradley brook. In the early 19th century Loudon laid out formal gardens nearer to the house. A stable-block stands 100 m. north-west of the site of the demolished house, and operated as a hotel from 1976 to 1998.[97] A walled garden with a glasshouse was laid out to the west of the house in the mid 18th century. A storage building adjoining the garden was given a second storey in the 19th century and adapted for use as a cottage.

Old Colwall

An Alice of Olde Colewall occurs in *c.*1288,[98] Adam of Oldecollewall in 1353,[99] and Thomas Baret of Old Colwall in 1588.[100] A William Brydges held land near the park in the first half of the 17th century.[101] This was perhaps William Brydges (d. 1627) of Upleadon (Herefs.),[102] whose fourth son Thomas (d. 1692) married as his second wife Catherine, the daughter of Thomas Barrett (d. 1658) at Old Colwall.[103] William Brydges (d. 1704),[104] the son of Thomas by his first wife, married his stepsister, Ursula, the daughter of Catherine and her first husband, John Drew of Dymock (Glos.). The estate passed to William and Ursula's son, also William (d. 1717),[105] who was succeeded in turn by his sons Richard (d. 1759) and Thomas (d. 1767),[106] whose heir was his son Richard (d. 1813).[107]

Under Richard's heir, Thomas (d. 1827),[108] the estate, comprising the mansion, two farms, and 385 a., was unsuccessfully put up for auction in 1819 and 1820.[109] It was

92 H. Colvin, *A Biographical Dictionary of British Architects, 1600–1840* (2008), 660; *ODNB*, s.v. Loudon, John Claudius, landscape gardener and horticultural writer (accessed 30 Sept. 2019).

93 *Worc. Jnl*, 21 Sept. 1962. Extant drawings, newspaper cuttings and photographs show the house prior to demolition: Historic England Archive, Architectural Red Box Collection, 1880/32–6.

94 HAS, K38/F/S2/32; *Heref. Times*, 9 Apr. 1910.

95 Milne and Ferguson, *Discover Colwall*, 24; NHLE, nos 1082143, Minaret, Boundary Walls and Gate Piers to North of Hope End Hotel; 1349711, Stableyard Gateway, Boundary Wall and Offices to south of Hope End Hotel (accessed 30 Sept. 2019).

96 Taylor, *Map of Herefs.* (1754).

97 NHLE, no. 1000276, Hope End (accessed 30 Sept. 2019); inf. from Mrs P. Hegarty.

98 HAS, AA59/A/1, p. 162.

99 HAS, AA26/II/27.

100 HAS, 037/5/38, will of James Shepherd 1588.

101 HAS, AE30/195.

102 John Burke, *Hist. Landed Gentry or Commoners of Great Britain and Ireland*, 4 vols (1833–8), IV, 552–4.

103 TNA, PROB 11/277/508; M.I. at Bosbury church.

104 TNA, PROB 11/479/480.

105 TNA, PROB 11/556/287; PROB 11/611/324.

106 TNA, PROB 11/846/343; HAS, will of Thomas Brydges, 30 May 1767.

107 HAS, AK99/12.

108 TNA, PROB 11/1727/354.

109 *Heref. Jnl*, 1 Dec. 1819; *Worc. Jnl*, 17 Aug. 1820.

offered again for sale in 1825,[110] and the retired banker James Martin was in possession by 1827.[111] When he died in 1870, at the age of 92,[112] the estate passed to his niece Elinor Treharne Holland, daughter of John Martin of Upper Hall in Ledbury.[113] She was the widowed second wife of Revd Frederick Whitmore Holland, whose first wife had been Elinor's cousin Penelope, daughter of Elinor's uncle Robert Martin. Elinor's son Edward Holland, who inherited the estate upon her death in 1903, was killed in action in 1916.[114] It then passed to his half-brother, Penelope's son Robert Martin Holland (d. 1944), chairman of the family bank, who assumed the surname Holland-Martin in 1917.[115] He resided at Overbury Court (Worcs.), and the estate was occupied by his daughter Julia, and her husband Algernon Cockburn Reyner-Wood (d. 1953).[116] She died in 1955, whereupon the estate descended to her nephew,[117] Christopher John Holland-Martin, deputy chairman of the family bank and MP for Ludlow, who died in 1960.[118] The whole estate, then comprising 611 a. and including the two farms, was offered for sale in 1963.[119] The house, stables and 135 a. of land were offered separately for sale in 1968,[120] and two rival concerns presented proposals to convert the estate into an animal park.[121] The house is currently occupied by the Trafford-Roberts family.

Old Colwall was built in the mid 18th century for the Brydges family, probably incorporating material from an earlier house on the same site.[122] Built on a rectangular plan, it comprises three parallel ranges, six bays wide and three storeys high constructed of brick, now roughcast, with hipped tile roofs. A large stack at the junction of the two rear ranges probably indicates the extent of the earlier house. A service wing of the late 18th or early 19th century was joined to the house by a late-19th-century two-storey service west wing. A 19th-century east wing was demolished c.1971. A separate stable block north-west of the house is dated 1840.[123]

Hoe Court

In 1577/8 Robert Hartland held a house called Hores,[124] and in the early 17th century the estate was held by Robert Hartland.[125] In 1620 the estate, comprising 208 a., passed from Hartland's son John to James Grove, the son of Robert Hartland's creditor, and by 1634 the estate, now comprising c.138 a., belonged to Thomas Woodyate, who sold it to

110 *Heref. Jnl,* 12 Oct. 1825.
111 HAS, AA26/I/2, pp. 42–4; Q/SR/115; *Heref. Jnl,* 23 May 1827, 2; J.B. Martin, *"The Grasshopper"* in *Lombard Street* (1892), 99–100.
112 *Worcs. Chron.* 7 Sept. 1870.
113 *Worcs. Chron.* 14 Feb. 1903.
114 *Glos. Echo,* 20 Sept. 1916.
115 *The Times,* 28 Jan. 1944.
116 *The Times,* 22 Oct. 1953.
117 GA, D2299/10598.
118 *The Times,* 6 Apr. 1960.
119 *The Times,* 25 Apr. 1963; CVS, F/113.
120 *The Times,* 11 Oct. 1968.
121 *Birmingham Daily Post,* 10 Mar. 1969.
122 NHLE, no. 1082147, Old Colwall (accessed 30 Sept. 2019); RCHME, *Inventory,* II, 54.
123 NHLE, no. 1082148, Service Quarters About 25 Yards North-West of Old Colwall (accessed 30 Sept. 2019).
124 HAS, AA59/A/2, f. 63.
125 TNA, C 2/JasI/H4/44.

Edmond Wrenford of Lyvers Ocle.[126] The estate was owned by John Hill of Bodenham in 1655, when it was purchased by Robert Bright (d. 1665) of Brockbury.[127] The estate subsequently passed to his eldest son Thomas (d. 1733), to his son Robert (d. 1770), and then to Robert Harcourt, Robert Bright's nephew by his sister Mary and her husband Peter Harcourt.[128] On Robert Harcourt's death in 1790, it passed to his widow Margaret and his son, another Robert.[129] The house was described as his residence when it was offered for sale in 1812, and again four years later.[130] Thomas Cook owned the house in the late 1820s, and he or a namesake were still there in 1841.[131]

Lt-Col Timothy Raper, a retired colonial officer, acquired the estate before 1851,[132] and he was probably responsible for the refurbishment of the house.[133] His son and heir, Robert William Raper, was a fellow and bursar of Trinity College, Oxford, where he resided.[134] Despite this, Raper played an instrumental role in the preservation of the Malvern Hills, securing the Malvern Hills Act of 1884, under which he acted as the first chairman of the conservators. He subsequently purchased the manorial rights of the manor of Barton Colwall.[135] Raper never married, and after his death in 1915 the estate passed to his sisters, Jean Ella (d. 1920) and Julia (d. 1921).[136] The estate was subsequently purchased by Thomas Wakefield Binyon, who died in 1930.[137] His daughter Elizabeth Muriel Binyon lived at Hoe Court until her death in 1967, when the house was again put up for sale.[138]

The present house dates from the mid 18th century, but was remodelled and extended in a 'Swiss-chalet Italianate style' in the mid 19th century.[139]

Hereford Cathedral

Money left to the cathedral chapter by Bishop Peter de Aigueblanche to establish an obit was used to acquire land and a windmill in Colwall, which in the late 13th century were let to Robert, vicar of Bishop's Frome.[140] The dean and chapter let half a yardland at 'Nesselynghope', in Barton Colwall, to John Nashe in 1475.[141] The chantry held land in the parish worth 17s. a year in 1547.[142]

---

126 HAS, D96/11.

127 HAS, D96/11.

128 HAS, D96/11; will of Thomas Bright, 9 Oct. 1733; will of Robert Bright, 25 July 1770.

129 TNA, PROB 11/1189/173; HAS, D96/11.

130 *Heref. Jnl,* 30 Sept. 1812; *Worc. Jnl,* 6 Feb. 1812; 15 Aug. 1816.

131 HAS, Q/REL/6/8/28-31; TNA, HO 107/424.

132 TNA, HO 107/1975.

133 Brooks and Pevsner, *Herefs.* 179; NHLE, no. 1082122, Hope Court (accessed 30 Sept. 2019).

134 *ODNB,* s.v. Raper, Robert William, college teacher and founder of university careers service (accessed 30 Sept. 2019).

135 Above, Barton Colwall.

136 *The Times,* 19 July 1915; 17 Feb. 1921; *National Probate Calendar* (Index of Wills and Administrations), 1920.

137 *The Times,* 1 July 1921; *London Gaz.* 15 Jan. 1932, p. 382.

138 *The Times,* 3 July 1968.

139 NHLE, no. 1000276, Hope End (accessed 30 Sept. 2019).

140 DCA 354; 2050. 'The will of Peter de Aqua Blanca Bishop of Heref. (1268)', ed. C. Eveleigh Woodruff, *Camden Soc.* 3rd sers. XXXVII (1926).

141 DCA 1908.

142 *Herefs. Chantry Valuations of 1547,* ed. M. Faraday (Walton-on-Thames, 2012), 9.

Priory of Little Malvern

In 1535 the priory of Little Malvern was in possession of estates worth 15*s*. 10*d* a year in rent.[143] These were granted in 1554 to William Bettys of Hadnam in the Isle of Ely (Cambs.) and Christopher Draper of London.[144] These were held by John Walwyn of Brockbury by 1571, by his son Robert in 1598, and subsequently descended with the manor of Brockbury.[145]

Priory of Great Malvern

The priory of Great Malvern was granted a portion of the tithes of Brockbury in 1271[146], previously held by Hugh de Furcis, a diocesan functionary.[147] This was presumably the origin of the belief that there was once a cell of the priory at Brockbury, for which there is no evidence.[148] The tithes amounted to 5*s*. a year in 1535.[149] Apparently rising in the detached part of the parish of Coddington, they were granted to Thomas Sheldon of Worcester and Laurence Poyner of Tewkesbury in 1544,[150] together with land in the parish in the tenure of John Ellis, presumably that described in 1535 as at Colowe, worth 4*s*. a year.[151]

143 Dugdale, *Mon.* IV, 455.
144 *Cal. Pat.* 1553–4, 336–7.
145 HAS, AE30/346–9; above, Brockbury.
146 *Reg. Swinfield*, 308.
147 *Reg. Cantilupe*, lxxi.
148 Dugdale, *Mon.* III, 447; Smith, *Malvern*, 59.
149 Dugdale, *Mon.* III, 452.
150 *L&P Hen. VIII*, XIX: 2, 186–7.
151 Dugdale, *Mon.* III, 452.

ECONOMIC HISTORY

AGRICULTURE FORMED THE BASIS OF Colwall's economy for most of its history, and the cultivation of fruit and hops was important from at least the 16th century. There was a mill at Colwall at the time of the Domesday survey and four mills exploited tributaries of the Cradley brook in later centuries, whilst there was also a windmill by the early 14th century. The quarrying of limestone and granite from the hillsides was also significant. The parish developed as a cultural resort after the arrival of the railway in the mid 19th century, carrying visitors attracted by the springs and scenery of the Malvern Hills. Bottling of the water began in the late 19th century. The Ballard family operated various enterprises in the parish including a brick and tile works, canning factory, vinegar brewery, and an ice works. Whilst the number of shops declined after the Second World War, in 2019 Colwall still has several cafés and shops, and the dramatic landscape continues to attract visitors to the parish.

Agriculture

Medieval and Early Modern Farming

From the 11th century (and before that time) until the early modern period most of the agricultural land in Colwall was farmed in numerous, relatively small tenant holdings. A survey *c.*1288 of the bishop's manor of Colwall listed 77 tenants, and there would also have been subtenants; for example there are likely to have been some subletting on Philip Ruddock's 4-yardland free holding.[1] The bishop's tenants between them cultivated more than 1,200 a. of land, five times the size of the bishop's demesne. Many of them were smallholders, with 38 per cent having 6 a. or less, sometimes no more than a house (messuage) and adjoining curtilage. Some 45 holdings, 58 per cent of the total, amounted to between 7 a. and 59 a. These tenants were living on quarter-yardlands (15 a.), half-yardlands (30 a.), or half-yardlands with some additional acres of forletland. Only one tenant held a full yardland (60 a.). These fractional units of tenancy were evidently the result of increasing demand for land, as the majority of half-yardlands appear in the survey as complete yardlands held by two tenants, suggesting a relatively recent division. The grain and legumes grown on these holdings would have provided the bread, ale and pottage needed for a family, while supplementary food and income came from the livestock kept on the abundant pasture, especially on the slopes of the Malvern Hills. A hint of extra resources available to tenants were the rents of honey and geese paid by most of the customary tenants. Those with limited land could have found

1   HAS, AA59/A/1, pp. 160–7.

some employment in agriculture, but also from quarrying, gathering furze, thorns and rushes from the commons, and from working in crafts such as the smith identified by his surname *c.*1288, and the one or two carpenters who paid poll tax in 1379.[2]

In the 14th and 15th centuries the reduced population was reflected in the combination of holdings to make larger units. In 1485 and 1496–7 tenants are recorded with 'two messuages and two half-yardlands', indicating the return of individuals cultivating about 60 a. of land, a quantity almost unknown in the late 13th century.[3] Ambitious tenants could also increase their acreage by obtaining parcels of demesne on lease. The larger units persisted after 1500, and multiple holdings (including one of three yardlands) appear in court rolls of 1555–6 and 1622, and in the survey of the late 16th century.[4] It became easier to hold extra land in the period 1350–1500 as rents fell, reflecting the declining demand for land, so that a half-yardland, for example, once rented for 15*s.* 10*d.*, was let in 1496–7 for 11*s.*[5] Tenures were also changed from the traditional customary land or copyhold to leasehold.

The combination of half-yardlands and yardlands could have increased the amount of land planted with crops, but another feature of the period was the expansion of pastoral farming by tenants, who paid to put their animals on the lord's pastures, including the park. The commons were also grazed more intensively, leading to a complaint in 1485 that a tenant was overburdening the common.[6]

Arable Fields

In 1086 there were a total of 13 ploughs and their teams of which two were on demesne. Ten were held by tenants (eight villeins and eight bordars) and one by a radman.[7] In 1240 six oxen and another draft animal were required to plough the demesnes of the bishop of Hereford's manor, suggesting only one plough was maintained on the bishop's farmland.[8] The survey of the bishop's manor *c.*1288 found that there were 231 a. of arable in his demesne.[9] In 1291 the bishop held one ploughland on his manor, and another two ploughlands belonged to the prebend of Barton Colwall.[10] In 1404 the demesne still consisted of one ploughland, valued at 5*s.* a year.[11]

The parish had numerous common or open fields in which different owners or tenants held strips. The extant records of the manor of Barton Colwall are far more extensive than those of the bishop's manor, and so it is possible to produce a clearer picture of agriculture in the south of the parish.[12] Not all of the fields can now certainly be identified. Several fields are first mentioned in the late 13th or early 14th centuries: West field, Combewell field, Wyngard field, South field, and Windmill field.

2   *Poll Taxes 1377–81*, ed. Fenwick, pt 1, 371.
3   HAS, AM33/2, 13.
4   HAS, AM33/6, 9; AA59/A/2, ff. 62v–66v.
5   HAS, AM33/13.
6   BL, Add. Roll 27311; HAS, AM33/2.
7   *Domesday*, 502.
8   *Reg. Swinfield*, 87.
9   HAS, AA59/A/1, p. 167; 'The Red Book', ed. Bannister, 24.
10   *Tax. Eccl.* (Rec. Com.), 168–9.
11   *Cal. Inq. Misc.* 1399–1422, 151.
12   HAS, AA26/II/1–41.

West field lay to the south of Cummins Farm, between Chance's Pitch and Petty France. Plots of land in the West field, divided into selions or small strips,[13] were recorded at places called '*Lattondine*' in 1332,[14] '*Uffcombe*' in 1339,[15] at '*Smaidole*' in 1353,[16] at '*Wassewallespol*' in 1353 and 1362,[17] and at '*Longland*' in 1353.[18] This latter presumably refers to the piece called Long Lands, on the north side of the road between Chance's Pitch and Petty France and still divided into strips in the 19th century.[19] In 1415 land in the field extended to Rodyate way, the modern road to Old Colwall.[20]

Combewell field, named for a well or spring, was first recorded *c*.1300 when five selions there adjoined the land of William of Brockbury.[21] In 1323 Combewell field lay next to Wyngard field,[22] and so can be identified with a close south of Cummins Farm called Comball in the 17th century which abutted land then called Wynyate,[23] and by the 19th century the Winnetts.[24] In 1372 it was called Wallefield.[25] Combewell and Wyngard fields may have been subdivisions of the large West field, or the three fields may have functioned together as part of a three-course rotation.

A South field, first recorded *c*.1300, lay alongside the road from the Barton to Hope,[26] and the common way to Dumbleton;[27] in 1353 a parcel of land lay in the field at 'le Wycheges'.[28] Windmill field, alongside the road from the Barton to Chance's Pitch and still described by that name in the 19th century,[29] was referred to in the 14th century.[30] The piece 'at the Rodyate' conveyed in 1272 probably lay in the West field,[31] and was not part of what was later called Great Rodyate field.[32] From the early 16th century there are references to Chadbrook field, which lay between the Rodyate and Colwall park.[33]

References to the common fields on the bishop's manor during the Middle Ages are elusive. Three undated deeds, probably of the late 13th century, refer to Hurst field,[34] which in the 19th century lay on the north side of Mill lane; Apleton,[35] modern Mapleton north of Hurst field; and Church field, east of the parish church.[36] Few traces of medieval

13   HAS, AA26/II/4.
14   HAS, AA26/II/19.
15   HAS, AA26/II/23.
16   HAS, AA26/II/25.
17   HAS, AA26/II/27, 31.
18   HAS, AA26/II/29.
19   HAS, L229.
20   HAS, AA26/II/35.
21   HAS, AA26/II/2–3, 5.
22   HAS, AA26/II/11, 14.
23   HAS, AA26/II/58.
24   HAS, L229.
25   HAS, AA26/II/23.
26   HAS, AA26/II/6.
27   HAS, AA26/II/30.
28   HAS, AA26/II/29.
29   HAS, L229.
30   HAS, AA26/II/18, 21.
31   HAS, AA26/II/I, 35.
32   HAS, L229.
33   HAS, AA26/II/41; AA59/A/2, ff. 78–9.
34   DCA 355.
35   HAS, AA26/II/7.
36   DCA 1412–3.

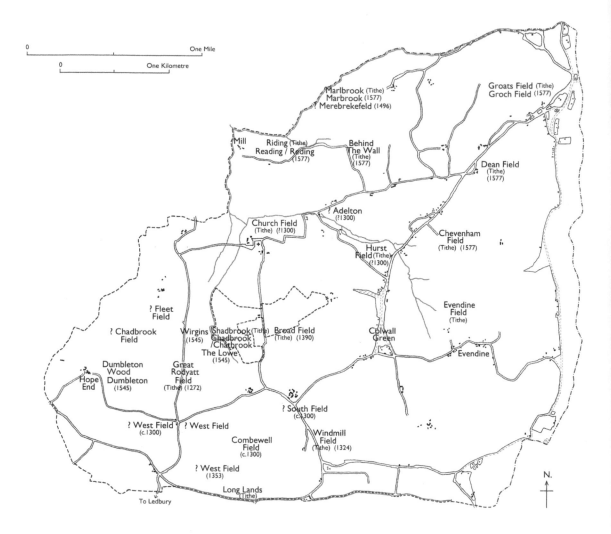

Map 2 Colwall common fields, with the dates when the individual field names were first recorded.

agriculture remain in the landscape in the north of the parish. Extensive evidence of medieval agriculture in the fields of the south of the parish gives further weight to the suggestion that much of the arable land in Colwall lay there,[37] although there are examples of ridge and furrow and strip lynchets near Park Farm and Old Colwall.[38] Other traces in the north of the parish may have been destroyed by the development of Colwall Stone.[39]

In the late 1570s a survey of the bishop's manor recorded that the tenants held land dispersed through a number of fields in the north and south of the parish.[40] Besides those fields already mentioned above, land was held in fields called Behind the Wall,

37   HER, 31918, 48811, 50057, 50059, 53267, 53553, 53581–3, 53585, 53592, 53595–6, 53599, 53603, 53610, 53612–5, 53621.
38   HER, 53589, 53591, 53601, 53611, 53616.
39   HER, 53620.
40   HAS, AA59/A/2, ff. 62v–81v.

Groats, Marbrook, and the Riding in the north; Chevenham and the Litticks in the east; Fleet, Maple and Winscombe in the south; and the unidentified Hanchorn and Nashend fields. All of the fields contained both customary and free land, although forlet land was concentrated on the church and the park. No single tenant held land in more than five fields, and holdings were unevenly distributed between the fields. George Pitt, for instance, held 2 a. in Wheatridge field, 3 a. in Horsecroft, 2 a. in Woodcroft, c.6 a. in Dean field, and c.6 a. on Maple Hill. Robert Gylding held c.18 a. in Chadbrook field, 7 a. in Fleet field, and c.4 a. in Hanchorn field.

Enclosure of the common fields appears to have been underway by the late 13th century, when land in Hurst field and at Mapleton was conveyed with hedges and ditches.[41] The eight selions of arable land in the unidentified 'Ballardduscroft' conveyed in 1351 may similarly have been held in severalty. Broad field, near the Wyche, was enclosed by hedges and ditches in 1390.[42] By the middle of the 16th century, two selions of arable land were enclosed next to Dean field, north-east of Colwall Stone.[43] An enclosure of 8 a. had been taken 'lately' from Chadbrook field in 1577, and a sheep house erected on the land.[44] Glebe terriers of the late 16th and early 17th centuries describe a number of enclosures, presumably ancient, which belonged to the rectory estate, including six enclosures amounting to 39 a. near the parsonage, another large enclosure east of Colwall Green, and at Marbrook field.[45] Strips in Church field appear to have been enclosed with hedges by the early 17th century.[46] Nevertheless, the glebe also consisted of strips of arable dispersed through the common fields of the parish. Piecemeal enclosure continued in the 17th and 18th centuries, but some common field land remained unenclosed into the 19th century.[47]

Colwall Park

There was an enclosure (*haia*) in the manor in 1086.[48] This could have become the bishop's park at Colwall, first definitely recorded in 1262, when it was broken into and the game hunted by Marcher lords in reprisal for the support of the bishop for Henry III.[49] Eight Colwall men were presented for illegally hunting game in the park c.1275.[50] The pasture within the park was valued at 30s. c.1288.[51] No game was recorded in the park in 1404 but its pasture was valued as 6s. 8d. for agistment, and pannage at 2s. a year.[52] The park was enlarged c.1500,[53] including land taken from Church field.[54] The

41   DCA 355, 1412–3.
42   DCA 351; HAS, AA26/II/24.
43   HAS, A72/1–2.
44   HAS, AA59/A/2, f. 79v.
45   HAS, HD2/1/27–9.
46   HAS, AM33/8.
47   BA, 31985[STG]/72; Eastnor Castle Archive, M1/14; HAS, R41/1; AK40/44; M5/44/17.
48   *Domesday*, 502.
49   *Cal. Pat.* 1258–66, 232; HER, 31680.
50   *Reg. Cantilupe*, 43.
51   HAS, AA59/A/1, p. 167; 'Red Book of Heref', 24.
52   *Cal. Inq. Misc.* 1399–1422, 151.
53   *Reg. Bothe*, 61.
54   TNA, SC 6/HENVIII/1511. An identical reduction in the value of herbage in Church field was noted in manorial accounts for 1496–7, but no reference was made to the enlargement of the park in that year: HAS, AM33/13.

park was held at farm in 1496–7,[55] and still in 1536–8.[56] During the 16th century, and probably before, the park was granted with the wardenship of the chase, to Richard Monnington in 1509, to Monnington and Edward Walwyn in 1510,[57] and to John Knotsford in 1563.[58] The park was said still to be stocked with deer in 1534,[59] but John Leland found none when he visited later in the decade.[60]

In 1572 Bishop John Scory let the manor with the park to his son Silvan Scory for three lives at a rent of £13 6s. 8d. a year.[61] In 1577 the park measured c.220 a., of which c.37 a. was enclosed with a pale and hedge but was usually mowed, and the remainder was converted to pasture or arable.[62] In 1586 John Scory's successor Herbert Westfaling complained to the Privy Council that the lease did not make the usual reservations for pasture and feeding of cattle and horses, arguing that the lease should be invalidated.[63] Following the abolition of episcopacy, the park was sold in 1648 to Thomas Alderman and John Flackett, but reverted to the bishop at the Restoration.[64] The park was still enclosed in 1664.[65] Traces of the park survived in field names in the 18th and 19th century, and boundary trees and the pale were still visible in the mid 19th century.[66]

The Bishop's Chase

A large area, perhaps as much as a third, of the parish lay within the bishop's chase, which extended south beyond the parish boundaries into the parishes of Eastnor and Bromsberrow. The boundary of the bishop's chase, also referred to as the Ledbury or Colwall Chase, were perambulated in 1277,[67] and 1577.[68] From a point called Primeswell, near the Wyche Cutting, it ran south along the Shire Ditch which divided it from Malvern Chase. From here it continued south to Bromsberrow and west to Eastnor, before returning north along the ridgeway. Re-entering Colwall parish at a point near Chance's Pitch, it continued north to the barton and Broadley (later Colwall) Green, from where it followed the highway back to Primeswell.

According to tradition, the chase was granted to the see of Hereford with other lands by Mildfrith, a 7th-century king of the Magonseate, a grant confirmed by Innocent II in the 12th century.[69] The chase was a source of friction with neighbouring lords, and an attractive target for the enemies of the bishops. Like the park, it was intruded upon by baronial opponents of the bishop c.1262.[70] Under Peter le Breton (bishop 1269–75),

55   HAS, AM33/13.
56   TNA, SC 6/HENVIII/1511.
57   *Reg. Mayew.* 89, 100.
58   Smith, *Malvern*, 134.
59   *L&P Hen. VIII*, VII, 465.
60   J. Leland, *Itinerary*, ed. Toulmin-Smith, V, 184.
61   HAS, AA59/A/2, ff. 89–89v.
62   HAS, AA59/A/2 f. 68.
63   *Acts of the Privy Council*, 1586–7, 101, 138.
64   BL, Add. MS 9049, f. 9v.
65   HAS, AA63/1, p. 156.
66   *Swinfield Accounts* (1854), clxviii.
67   HAS, AA59/A/1, p. 145.
68   HAS, AA59/A/2 f. 103.
69   *Fasti Eccles. Ang.* 1066–1300, VIII, xxi.
70   *Cal. Pat.* 1258–66, 232.

the chase was appropriated by Gilbert de Clare, 7th earl of Gloucester, the lord of the neighbouring Malvern Chase. The bishop apparently made no effort to resist this encroachment, but his successor Thomas de Cantilupe immediately initiated a suit to restore his rights.[71] After delays of three years, a jury found for the bishop and his rights over his chase were restored.[72] Consequently the earl had the Shire Ditch, probably a prehistoric boundary,[73] renewed to serve as a boundary between his chase and the bishop's.[74] The chase was placed in the custody of Alexander Lillisford when bishop Orleton's estates were confiscated in 1324.[75]

In 1277 the bishop employed a forester at Colwall, who was to give the bishop each year 12 hens, worth 16*d.*, and 100 eggs, worth 3*d.*, in return for wood at Christmas.[76] The chase provided Bishop Swinfield with venison out of season in 1290,[77] and he and his retinue hunted in it during both stays at Colwall in that year.[78] A number of men, including six tenants of the manor of Barton Colwall, were convicted in 1286 of hunting in the chase and taking a deer.[79] In 1394 four men were accused of hunting in the chase at Colwall and Ledbury, taking fee-bucks and fee-does.[80] Similarly, Colwall men were presented for hunting in Malvern chase in 1338, 1340, 1344, and 1347.[81] Grants of the keepership of the chase were made to John Ewyas in 1378,[82] John Baynham in 1409,[83] Walter Corbet of Cowley in 1435,[84] and Sir Walter Devereux in 1458.[85] In 1509 the bishop granted the custody of his chase and park to Richard Monnington, and in the following year to Monnington and Edward Walwyn,[86] perhaps in reversion, as Monnington was still the keeper in 1534.[87] John Knotsford of Hanley Castle (Worcs.) was appointed keeper in 1562 by Bishop Scory,[88] presumably in his last act as lord of the chase.

Under the Act of Exchange of 1559,[89] Scory was required in 1562 to exchange a number of his estates for tithes belonging to the Crown. The Bishop's Chase passed to the Crown with Ledbury manor at this time, the bishop retaining a walk with a keeper's place, and two fee-bucks and two-fee does each year. A decision was made to disafforest the Bishop's Chase simultaneously with Malvern Chase, held by the Crown since the late 15th century.[90] A plan of the two chases produced in 1628 depicts a much-diminished

71 *Reg. Cantilupe*, 23.
72 *Reg. Cantilupe*, 34, 59–62, 227.
73 Above, Colwall Parish, Landscape.
74 Smith, *Malvern*, 31; Ray, *Archaeology of Herefs.* 106.
75 *Cal. Pat.* 1321–4, 403.
76 HAS, AA59/A/1, p. 164.
77 *Expenses of Swinfield*, LIX, 71.
78 *Expenses of Swinfield*, LIX, 72, 108.
79 *Reg. Swinfield*, 112–3.
80 *Reg. Trefnant*, 164.
81 *Cal. Pat.* 1338–40, 183; 1340–43, 97; 1343–5, 288; 1345–8, 307.
82 *Reg. Gilbert*, 6.
83 *Reg. Mascall*, 72–3.
84 *Reg. Spofford*, 207.
85 *Reg. Stanbury*, 46.
86 *Reg. Meyew*, 89, 100.
87 *L&P Hen. VIII*, VII, 465.
88 HAS, AA59/A/2, ff. 103v–4v.
89 1 Eliz. I c.19.
90 *Cal. Pat.* 1560–3, 284–9; HAS, AA59/A/2, ff. 215–31; Smith, *Malvern*, 26–7.

bishop's chase, or 'Collaway common', comprising *c*.355 a., including a portion north of the road from Wyche Cutting, marked the 'Herefordshire Purlew' and measuring *c*.50 a.[91] Commissioners were appointed to enquire into the matter *c*.1630,[92] as a result of which Bishop Godwin may have made an effort to reassert his rights over the bishop's chase.[93] Nevertheless, the chase was disafforested in the following year, with several parcels claimed by the king of which seven were in Colwall and known collectively as the King's third, and the remaining land allotted to the lords of the manors.[94]

The King's third was sold to Sir Cornelius Vermuyden,[95] who sold it to Sir Richard Heath,[96] who sold it in turn to Sir William Russell of Strensham (Worcs.) and George Strode of Squerries (Kent).[97] A second plan of the chases, produced in 1633 as part of the process of allotting the King's third, marks a plot measuring *c*.29 a. laid out within Colwall common.[98] A survey of 1650 found a parcel of land in Colwall measuring *c*.37 a. had been allotted to the King and enclosed in 1633, but subsequently it had been thrown open and used as part of the common.[99] The land together with all rights of hunting, hawking, fowling and fishing within the former chase were sold in 1650 by the trustees for Crown lands to William Rysell of Gloucester,[100] but the land reverted to its previous owners at the Restoration, confirmed by an Act of Parliament in 1664.[101] Strode's son Nicholas was in possession of the Crown's third in Colwall in 1675, when he let it to Rowland Pitt for a term of 21 years.[102] The walk within the chase that had been allotted to the bishop in 1562 was sold by the trustees for the sale of bishops' lands in 1654 to John Birch of Whitbourne.[103] These were presumably the lands which continued to be held by Birch under a lease from the bishop after the Restoration, and which bishop Gilbert Ironside let to his son Robert for three lives in 1698.[104] Ironside assigned the remainder of his lease to Sir George Strode in 1703.[105]

Meadow and Pasture

Only 8 a. of meadow were recorded belonging to the manor in 1086, almost certainly an underestimate, as the survey of *c*.1288 recorded 26 a. of meadow and *c*.11 a. of pasture in the demesne, not including the park.[106] Meadow lined Colwall's numerous streams and brooks, and a reference to '*le Flodegatemeduwe*' in a deed of the late 13th century may indicate that there were water meadows in the parish at that date.[107] These perhaps

91 Society of Antiquaries, MS 520/VI/5 68.2. E.A.B. Barnard, *Trans of the Worcs. Arch. Soc.* (1929), 137–41.
92 TNA, E 178/5982; E 178/7306.
93 *Cal. S.P. Dom.* 1629–31, 486.
94 *Cal. S.P. Dom.* 1631–33, 285; TNA, SP 17/B/9; SP 16/214, f. 18a.
95 *Cal. S.P. Dom.* 1629–31, 353.
96 *Cal. S.P. Dom.* 1636–7, 211.
97 Smith, *Malvern*, 155.
98 WAAS, X705:24 BA81/366.
99 TNA, E 317/HEREF/18.
100 TNA, E 320/F24.
101 16 Chas. II c.v.
102 Herts. Archives and Local Studies, DE/K/46834.
103 HAS, O57/6.
104 Herts. Archives and Local Studies, DE/K/46836.
105 Herts. Archives and Local Studies, DE/K/46837, 46875.
106 *Domesday*, 502; HAS, AA59/A/1, p. 167.
107 DCA 355.

lay along the Chevenham brook, particularly near the Upper Colwall and Lugg's mills. Hurst moor, at the far end of Hurst field and first referred to in the late 13th century, was presumably another meadow lying next to Chevenham brook.[108] A number of undated earthworks to the south of Brockhill farm are suggestive of the channels, drains, sluices and ponds of a water meadow.[109]

Colwall was probably typical of Herefordshire in having a corn-cattle farming economy by the late 16th century. In the south of the parish in particular, pasture grounds encircling common fields are suggestive of an infield-outfield system. Comyn's moor and Uffcombes Green, adjoining Combewell and West fields respectively, were both mentioned in the 14th century.[110] Richard Bromefeld, prebendary of Barton Colwall 1492–1518,[111] enclosed two carucates (*aratra*) of land within his manor.[112] These were presumably the former common fields south of Cummins farm, much of which had been enclosed and converted to permanent pasture by the early 17th century.[113] By the late 18th century, the parish was said to be divided almost equally between arable and pasture, not including the former chase on the west side of the Malvern Hills.[114]

The herbage within the bishop's meadows and park was demised to several tenants for c.£4 a year in 1496–7,[115] rising to more than £6 by 1536–8.[116] The rector was entitled to a crop of hay from a small meadow east of the parish church in the late 16th century,[117] and held pieces in other meadows, which may have been dole meadows. The survey of 1577 records that most tenants held meadow and pasture with their arable land.[118]

Colwall's tenants had common of pasture in the Bishop's Chase,[119] and by the early 14th century they paid for the agistment a rent of 5 qtrs of oats each year to the lord of Hanley Castle (Worcs.) for common in Malvern Chase.[120] In the 16th century they paid an annual fixed rent of 8 qtrs of oats, hens and eggs.[121] In 1540 Colwall tenants were ordered by Hanley manor court not to drive their cattle into Malvern chase,[122] an order reiterated later in the century.[123] By the early 17th century, and presumably before, tenants had Lammas rights in the fields called Old Grove, Veldiat, and Hanchorn.[124]

---

108 DCA 355.

109 *PastScape*, no. 1334860.

110 HAS, AA26/II/13, 23, 28.

111 *Fasti Eccles. Ang. 1300–1541*, II, 19.

112 I.S. Leadam, 'The Inquisition of 1517. Inclosures and evictions. Edited from the Lansdowne MS. I. 153. Part II', *Trans. Royal Hist. Soc.* n.s. VII (1893), 264.

113 HAS, AE30/364.

114 HAS, CF50/243.

115 HAS, AM33/13.

116 TNA, SC 6/HENVIII/1511.

117 HAS, HD2/1/27–9.

118 HAS, AA59/A/2.

119 HAS, AA59/A/2, f. 88v.

120 J.P. Toomey, 'A medieval woodland manor: Hanley Castle, Worcestershire', unpubl. PhD thesis, Univ. of Birmingham (1997), 51. *Cal. Inq. p.m.* 1307–16, 328; TNA, C 134/42/1.

121 Smith, *Malvern*, 39.

122 M.G. Watkins, *Collections towards the History and Antiquities of the County of Hereford, in Continuation of Duncumb's History*, IV (1902), 56; WAAS, 705:79 BA1533.

123 WAAS, 705:24 BA81, 352.

124 HAS, AM33/9.

Woodland

In 1086 there was no wood recorded.[125] The survey of 1577 noted good timber on some of the customary tenements, but did not record any coppices or woods within the parish.[126] John Hartland's estate at the Hores included two coppices which together measured 16 a. in 1616.[127] In 1686 Rowland Pitt's share of woodland at Perry Croft amounted to 20 a., and part of a 6-a. leasow was also woodland.[128] His possessions at his death included 13 tons of rough oak timber, two ash trees, and 7 tons of ash timber. Thomas Bright's lands in 1725 included a piece of woodland called Ackhorne Coppice.[129] In 1750 Richard Bridges of Old Colwall conveyed arable land with an adjoining coppice, to the east of Sparrow Hill wood or coppice.[130] At the end of the century, John Duncumb recorded that there was little timber grown in the parish, but what was grown was mainly oak.[131] Coppice woodlands on the southern boundary of Colwall parish measuring a total of *c.*12 a. belonged to the Eastnor estate.[132] Other coppices at Petty France and Sparrow Hill belonged to Richard Brydges of Old Colwall, who responded to the increased demand for wood during the Napoleonic Wars by advertising 289 trees, mainly oaks, in 1796, and another 187 timber trees in 1798.[133] Ninety-nine trees belonging to the Malt House were offered for sale in May 1824.[134]

Crops and Livestock

The evidence of extant probate records from the 16th century onwards record the cultivation of wheat, barley, oats, and muncorn (a mixture of different grains sown together); peas and other fodder crops were also sown. Wheat appears to have been the principal corn crop, and was often listed stored in houses or barns or growing in the ground. In the mid 18th century a three-course rotation, of wheat, Lent grain, and fallow, was still being practised.[135] Wheat was often cultivated alongside other crops by the tenants of Colwall. John Barston died with 6 cwt of hops in his possession in 1671, valued at £12, and the gentleman Rowland Pitt had a 6-a. leasow sown partly with hops in 1686, and was owed £34 for hops.[136] Other inventories refer to smaller amounts of hops.[137] In 1691 Robert Bright of Brockbury mortgaged 6 a. of pasture part of which had

125 *Domesday*, 502.
126 HAS, AA59/A/2, ff. 71, 76v, 79.
127 HAS, D96/11.
128 HAS, 94/1/30, inventory of Rowland Pitt, 1686.
129 HAS, O14/3, will of Thomas Bright, 1725.
130 HAS, AA26/II/52.
131 HAS, CF50/243.
132 Eastnor Castle Archive, Map of Eastnor Estate, 1832.
133 *Heref. Jnl,* 4 May 1796; 2 May 1798.
134 *Heref. Jnl,* 19 May 1824.
135 HAS, AE30/70.
136 HAS, 29/2/31, inventory of John Barston, 1670; 94/1/30, inventory of Rowland Pitt, 1686.
137 HAS, X2/5/6, inventory of William Brook, 1661; 19/3/16, inventory of Edmond Dangerfield, 1668; X2/5/20, inventory of Mary Hall, 1676; X2/5/13, inventory of Robert Hussie, 1684; X2/5/14, inventory of John Pillinger, 1684; 128/4/3, inventory of Joseph Hartland, 1697.

previously been planted with hops.[138] Hemp and flax are recorded at the start and end of the 17th century;[139] a field near Hoars was called Flax Close in 1616.[140]

The abundant pasture of the parish enabled the inhabitants to combine maintaining large numbers of livestock with cultivating arable land. Draught oxen were recorded in 21 extant wills and inventories proved at Hereford between 1544 and 1725. In 1567 Thomas Gilding had three oxen called Whitehorn, Brown and Browning; in 1686 Rowland Pitt had eight oxen.[141] William Brook, a yeoman who died in 1661, had corn, malt, peas, hops, and other grain in his house and barn, five oxen and bullocks, 16 cattle, five calves, two mares and three colts, 14 sheep, 12 pigs, and poultry.[142] In 1670 John Unett had 3 a. of land sown with wheat, 11 cattle, three yearlings, four calves, two mares, two colts, 20 sheep, and an unspecified number of pigs.[143] William Hill, who died in 1675, left 12 a. of corn on the ground and 4 a. more to sow, more corn and pulses in the barn, eight cows and a bull, six heifers, seven calves, 48 sheep, three mares and a colt, and eight pigs.[144] The spinster Mary Hall bequeathed 16 bushels of corn, 40 bushels of pulse, and a parcel of spoiled hops; her livestock comprised five cows, two heifers, six calves, two mares and a nag, and nine pigs in 1676.[145]

Dairying was an important activity, and references to the production of butter and cheeses are numerous. In 1670 John Unett's herd included 11 milk cows.[146] Cheese presses are recorded in the inventories of five late-17th-century parishioners, as well as cheese rings, churns, cheese vats, and other dairying equipment.[147] A 'deyer board' was recorded in the early 17th century,[148] and 11 inventories or wills refer to butteries, dairies or dey-houses.[149] Sheep were kept on both a small and large scale, and inventories often list a quantity of wool and woollen yarn, as well as spinning-wheels. In addition to his 20 sheep, John Unett's possessions included wool, yarn, and a woollen wheel. William Hill had 48 sheep and about four or five stones of wool worth £1 10s., two little linen wheels and a woollen wheel.[150] Joseph Hartland had a flock of 42 sheep and wool worth £3, and John Nelme had 53 sheep and wool valued at £2 8s.[151] Pigs are recorded in most

138 HAS, AE30/169.
139 HAS, 9/3/2, will of William Eckley, 1607; 126/6/10, will of John Nelme, 1697.
140 HAS, D96/11.
141 HAS, 18/3/6, will of Thomas Gilding, 1567; X2/5/6, inventory of William Brook, 1661; 18/4/8, inventory of Richard Pitt, 1667; 61/2/40, inventory of John King, 1679; 94/1/30, inventory of Rowland Pitt, 1686.
142 HAS, X2/5/6, inventory of William Brook, 1661.
143 HAS, 26/2/40, inventory of John Unett, 1670.
144 HAS, 44/2/21, inventory of William Hill, 1675.
145 HAS, X2/5/20, inventory of Mary Hall, 1676.
146 HAS, 26/2/40, inventory of John Unett, 1670.
147 HAS, 19/3/16, inventory of Edmond Dangerfield, 1668; 44/2/21, inventory of William Hill, 1675; X2/5/20, inventory of Mary Hall, 1676; 83/1/16, inventory of Richard Mason, 1683; 105/1/12, inventory of John Hooper, 1688.
148 HAS, 8/3/14, will of Robert Bastone, 1606.
149 HAS, 26/2/40, inventory of John Unett, 1640; 18/4/3, inventory of Richard Hall, 1662; 13/2/21, inventory of William Hill, 1667; 26/2/40, inventory of John Unett, 1670; X2/5/20, inventory of Mary Hall, 1676; 61/2/40, inventory of John Hill, 1679; 83/1/16, inventory of Richard Mason, 1683; 94/1/30, inventory of Rowland Pitt, 1686; 126/6/10, inventory of John Nelme, 1697; 128/4/3, inventory of Joseph Hartland, 1697; O14/3, will of Thomas Bright, 1725.
150 HAS, 44/2/21, inventory of William Hill, 1675.
151 HAS, 126/6/10, inventory of John Nelme, 1697; 128/4/3, inventory of Joseph Hartland, 1697.

of the wills and inventories of the 16th and 17th centuries. Thomas Gilding in 1567 and William Eckley in 1607 both bequeathed store pigs.[152] Henry Wright had two sows and seven pigs in 1667, Richard Pitt a sow and four store pigs, also in 1667, and John Hancocks a sow, pigs and a store pig in 1675.[153]

Even those with small estates could maintain livestock because of the abundant commons within the parish. Edward Stone, a labourer who made his will in 1605, bequeathed two cows, nine sheep and five lambs among his possessions.[154] Richard Hall, also described as a labourer, referred to his garden and pasture but not to any arable land in his will of 1662.[155] At his death he possessed one cow and 14 sheep. In 1682 a man with ½ a. of corn on ground and less than two bushels in total of corn, barley and pulse in his house also possessed two ewes and two lambs.[156] Craftsmen supplemented their trades by maintaining livestock. In 1598 a smith included nine sheep and five lambs among his bequests.[157] The mason Richard Mason, who died in 1683, owned ½ a. of corn on the ground, two cows and 27 sheep.[158] Robert Hussie, a corvisor who died in 1684, owned two cattle, one colt, two pigs, and some hops, and John Hussey, also a corvisor and possibly his son, owned sheep when he died two years later.[159] A carpenter who died in 1685 possessed a cow, two heifers, one calf, and some sheep.[160]

Eight orchards were recorded on the bishop's manor in 1577,[161] and several inventories refer to cider mills.[162] John Barston's inventory recorded cider and perry worth £5 in 1670. William Hill had eight hogshead of cider and perry, worth £5 6s. 8d., for the use of his household in 1675, and Rowland Pitt had three hogshead of cider and seven of perry, worth £4, in 1686.[163] In 1606 Robert Bastone bequeathed a stall of bees to each of his four daughters, and in 1670 John Barston had four hives of bees valued at 4s.[164]

During the 18th and 19th centuries the abundant pasture ensured that animal husbandry continued to take precedence, and the numbers of cattle within the parish may have been swollen by the arrival of animals to be fattened for markets at Ledbury and Hereford. Nevertheless, large numbers were also bred in the parish. A sale of stock at Oldcastle Farm in 1825 included 18 heifers, 17 milch cows, 16 steers, six yearling bullocks and heifers, 12 rearing calves, two feeding calves and five young bulls, while

152 HAS, 18/3/6, will of Thomas Gilding, 1567; 9/3/2, will of William Eckley, 1607.
153 HAS, 13/2/9, inventory of Henry Wright, 1667; 18/4/8, inventory of Richard Pitt, 1667; X2/5/19, inventory of John Hancocks, 1675.
154 HAS, 8/3/2, will of Edward Stone, 1605.
155 HAS, 18/4/3, will and inventory of Richard Hall, 1662.
156 HAS, X2/5/11, inventory of John Hackett, 1682.
157 HAS 9/3/77, will of James Brooke, 1598.
158 HAS, 83/1/16 inventory of Richard Mason, 1683.
159 HAS, X2/5/13, inventory of Robert Hussie, 1684; X2/5/12, inventory of John Hussey, 1686.
160 HAS, 92/1/4, inventory of Richard Ockley, 1685.
161 HAS, AA59/A/2, ff. 62v–81v.
162 HAS, 13/2/9, inventory of Henry Wright, 1667; 19/3/16, inventory of Edmond Dangerfield, 1668; 29/2/31, inventory of John Barston, 1671; 44/2/21, inventory of William Hill, 1675; X2/5/20, inventory of Mary Hall, 1676; 61/2/40, inventory of John King, 1679; 90/2/2, inventory of John James, 1685; 92/1/4 inventory of Richard Ockley, 1685; 94/1/30, inventory of Rowland Pitt, 1686.
163 HAS, 29/2/31, inventory of John Barston, 1670; 44/2/21, inventory of William Hill, 1675; 94/1/30, inventory of Rowland Pitt, 1686
164 HAS, 8/3/14, will of Robert Bastone, 1606; 29/2/31, inventory of John Barston, 1671.

a sale at Lodge Farm in 1834 included 46 'prime useful cattle'.[165] Breeding horses was also common: at Brockhill Farm in 1833 the animals for sale included two mares in foal, a yearling filly, and a suckling filly; a year later there were 15 horses for sale at Lodge Farm.[166] Substantial numbers of sheep were recorded in the parish in the early 19th century, including 260 at Upper House, Evendine in 1802, 100 at Cummins Farm in 1811, 426 at Oldcastle Farm in 1825, 229 at Oldcastle Farm in 1829, and 116 at the Winnings in 1832.[167] Access to large quantities of manure should have ensured that arable yields were usually high. The need to sustain the animals through the winter necessitated the planting of large amounts of fodder crops, including vetches, beans, cabbages, potatoes, and perhaps also the barley.[168] Hops and orcharding were prominent, and flax continued to be grown within the parish. Charles Lucy grew 137 stone of flax c.1788, and William Skipp grew 134 stones and Thomas Barrett 36 stones c.1791.[169]

Farming from 1800

From the mid 19th century new farm buildings were built and existing ones improved, partly the result of improvements in the housing of livestock, increasing numbers of cattle kept, and the size of farms.[170] In particular, three model farmsteads date from this period. The first, Barton Farm, was a substantial brick farm built on a new site at Chance's Pitch c.1850. Winnings Farm was built by Stephen Ballard in 1863, apparently without a threshing barn because steam engines drove portable threshing machines instead.[171] The farm was demolished in the late 20th century. Modern farm buildings were built at Park Farm, previously known as Lodge farm, in 1867 to the north of the ancient farmstead, comprising a brick-built range of cattle sheds, milking parlour, a feeding yard, a machine shed, and two large barns.[172] Elsewhere, modern farm buildings updated existing farmsteads, for example by the construction of open-fronted sheds for yard cattle, often with timber posts to the front. The wide-span cow house at Netherpath Farm was unusual for the area, with a central feeding passage the length of the building.[173] The stone barn at Hoe Court was probably intended as a decorative feature when viewed from the house.[174]

In 1839 the assistant tithe commissioner found a three-course crop rotation still in use in the parish, and the soil of poor quality, mainly comprising a stiff clay.[175] A total

---

165 *Heref. Jnl*, 19 Oct. 1825; 22 Oct. 1834.

166 *Heref. Jnl*, 13 Nov. 1833; 22 Oct. 1834.

167 *Heref. Jnl*, 24 Feb. 1802; 1 May 1811; 19 Oct. 1825; 4 July 1832.

168 *Heref. Jnl*, 13 Jan. 1830; 4 July 1832; 1 Aug. 1832; 13 Nov. 1833; 22 Oct. 1834.

169 *Heref. Jnl*, 22 Aug. 1790; 15 Dec. 1790; 14 Nov. 1792; 19 Oct. 1825.

170 J.E.C. Peters, unpubl. report on Colwall farm buildings; idem, 'The barns of eastern Herefs.', in *Essays in Honour of Jim and Muriel Tonkin* (2011), 117–28; idem., 'Stables in eastern Herefs.', *TWNFC*, 61 (2013), 86–94.

171 Photograph seen in an exhibition at the village hall, Colwall, Apr. 1995; HAS, B10/11; P. Hurle, *Stephen Ballard*, 80, 82; Ballard, *Colwall Collection*, 44; HER, 46816.

172 Brookes and Pevsner, *Herefs.* 177; HAS, R41/1; AK40/44; M5/44/17; CN37/293; HER, 42741; 46819.

173 HER, 46829.

174 HER,46814

175 TNA, IR 18/3010.

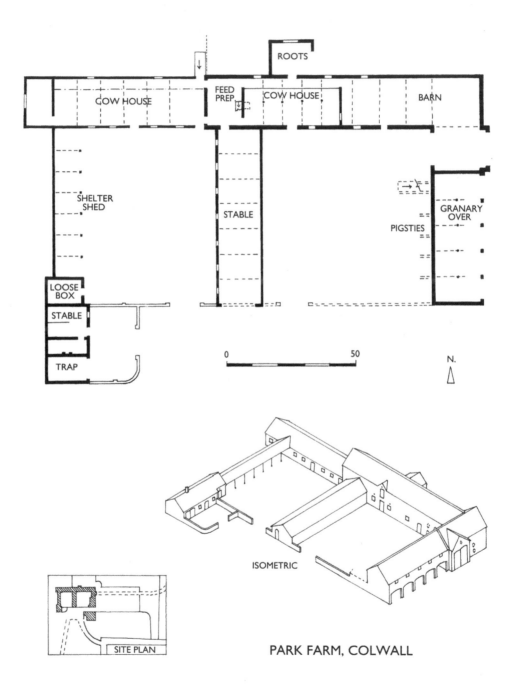

ROOTS

COW HOUSE

FEED PREP

COW HOUSE

BARN

SHELTER SHED

STABLE

GRANARY OVER

PIGSTIES

LOOSE BOX

STABLE

TRAP

0   50

N.

ISOMETRIC

SITE PLAN

PARK FARM, COLWALL

Figure 17 *Plan of Colwall Park Farm drawn by J.E.C. Peters.*

of 2,773 a. were being farmed, of which 712 a. were under crops. Almost half of this total, 340 a., was sown with wheat in 1839, 82 a. with barley, 50 a. with oats, 90 a. with peas, 30 a. with potatoes, and 50 a. with hops; another 50 a. lay under clover. There was little permanent meadow in the parish, with the pasture being alternately mown and grazed. In 1839 1,221 a. was recorded as pasture and another 610 a. were meadow. The assistant commissioner recorded a total of 157 cows, 86 calves, and 457 ewes, although he expressed considerable reservation about the accuracy of his figures. There were 180 a. of coppices, and an unknown acreage of orchards.

In 1851 the census enumerators recorded 22 farms and smallholdings, ranging in size from 3 a. to 300 a., farming a total of 2,523 a.[176] Four farms were larger than 200 a., of which the largest was Park Farm with 300 a., held on a lease from the bishop by Henry Peyton, who employed 16 men. Other large farms included Old Castle 252 a., Brockbury 213 a. and Barton Court 206 a. A further nine farms were between 100 a. and 200 a. in size. These 13 farms employed a total of 65 men, with 16 employed at Park Farm. During the 1850s two publicans and a shopkeeper combined their occupations with farming smallholdings. In 1911 no farm within the parish exceeded 200 a., and there were nine farms with more than 100 a., of which Park Farm was still the largest, with c.186 a. By 1941 there were 42 holdings in Colwall, covering a total of c.2,999 a.[177] The largest farm was Old Colwall with c.518 a., followed by Grovesend with c.267 a. Nine other farms were between 100 a. and 200 a., and there were 16 small holdings with between 5 a. and 20 a., cultivated by individuals whose principal occupation was not farming. Those classified as 'full-time farmers' generally worked 80 a. of land or more. Approximately three-fifths of the land was occupied and farmed by the owners.

Wheat remained the principal crop, although its cultivation fluctuated in the century after 1851,[178] declining from c.384 a. in 1875 to just 53 a. in 1931, before increasing again during the Second World War, to c.184 a. in 1941, and 313 a. in 1946, after which it remained at just over 200 a. Barley, oats, beans and potatoes also were grown in smaller amounts, together with turnips, mangolds, vetches or tares. The number of milk cows and heifers remained about the same in the late 19th and early 20th centuries in the range of 180 and 250. Sheep numbers ranged from under 300 ewes to over 1,000, producing between 600 and 1,000 lambs annually. There was an increase in sheep farming in the 1930s. Likewise the number of pigs increased in the late 19th and early 20th centuries from 150–300 in the latter decades of the 19th to over 600 in the late 1930s. In 1881 there were 99 individuals employed in agriculture, of which 26 were farmers and their families.[179] The total number of people working in agriculture in the 20th century peaked in 1946 at 127, falling to 101 by 1956, and continuing to decline over the second half of the century. The number of cattle and sheep has increased whilst the number of pigs has declined. Arable farming remains important particularly for the growing of wheat, barley, oats, mixed corn and potatoes and farm size has increased. Some smaller holdings survive and land is both owned and rented.

176 This paragraph is based on TNA, HO 107/1975; RG 11/2581; HAS, AG9/51, passim, and maps 36/2, 5–6, 9–10.
177 This paragraph based on TNA, MAF 32/5/151; MAF 73/17/36.
178 This paragraph is based on a five-year sampling of TNA, MAF 68.
179 Census, 1881.

Hops

The earliest surviving hop kilns in the parish are at Colwall Mill farm and date from the 18th century, and there are references to hop-yards at Brockbury in 1818.[180] In 1824 there were 119 a. of hops grown at Colwall, a comparatively small amount for its size.[181] By 1839 this had fallen to just 50 a.[182] Nevertheless, hops continued to be cultivated in the parish, and Brockbury, Cummins and Hope End farms were marked on a map of hop-growing districts in Herefordshire and Worcestershire in the 1890s.[183] The south end of the barn at Cummins Farm was converted for hop-drying in the late 19th century, with a square kiln added to the side.[184]

Orchards

Although the assistant tithe commissioner was unable to calculate the total acreage of orchards within the parish, the final apportionment recorded numerous small orchards,[185] and field names give a further indication of the importance of orcharding within the parish.[186] Cider was often mentioned among the miscellaneous items listed in the sale of farming equipment. The commodities for sale at Old Colwall in 1820 included 1,500 gallons of 'exceeding rich cider and perry, fit for bottling'. At Oldcastle Farm in 1825, where the farmer was probably producing cider on a commercial scale, a distinction was drawn between 5 hogshead of 'prime cider' and 6 hogshead of 'family cider'. Amongst the rest of the goods for sale were 12 cider hairs, three 500-gallon pipes, one 400-gallon pipe, and one 200-gallon pipe, as well as 42 empty hogsheads and other casks.[187]

The opening of the railway in 1861 led to an increase in fruit production. The engineer Stephen Ballard (d. 1890) established a large fruit farm and a cider vinegar factory.[188] Orchards of cherries, damsons, apples and pears had been planted alongside Old Church Road by 1885, and the avenues of lime trees which are characteristic of the village were also planted to attract bees to the orchards.[189] In the early 20th century the local labourers were supplemented by the arrival of women from industrial areas such as Dudley (Worcs.) to undertake seasonal work picking fruit.[190] Stephen Ballard (d. 1952) began experimenting with fruit bottling during the First World War, and later introduced canning at Grovesend Farm.[191] His customers included Boots, Cadbury's and Terry's of York, and the main markets for the fruit were in Birmingham, South Wales, Manchester and Liverpool.[192] Between the First and Second World Wars and at the height of the

180 *Heref. Jnl,* 7 Oct. 1818.
181 *Account of Number of Acres under Cultivation for Hops, 1824* (Parl. Papers, 1825 (52), xx), p. 3.
182 TNA, IR 18/3010.
183 *Map of the Hop-Growing Districts of Worcs. and Herefs. Compiles by J.W. Buckland & Co.* (1890), BL, Maps 5800 (14.).
184 J.E.C. Peters, unpubl. report on Colwall farm buildings.
185 TNA, IR 18/3010.
186 HAS, AA26/III/2; R41/1; M5/44/17; AL59/1; CK23/61.
187 *Heref. Jnl,* 19 Oct. 1825.
188 *ODNB,* s.v. Ballard, Stephen, civil engineer (accessed 30 Sept. 2019).
189 Ballard, *Colwall Collection.*
190 HAS, AW86/2, 54.
191 Ballard, *Colwall Collection,* 23.
192 HAS, AW86/2, p. 56.

season the fruit business employed around 150 pickers.[193] In 1936 there were 387 a. of orchards, including *c.*57 a. of small fruit.

Fruit production declined after the Second World War. From the late 1950s the height of the trees and quality of fruit reduced the productivity and profit of the business.[194] The canning factory closed in 1961 and the apple packing shed was rented to Geoffrey Knight, who developed several Colwall varieties including the Captain Tom apple and the Golden Glow apricot.[195] There has been a revival of orcharding in the early 21st century, and an orchard group established in Colwall in 2007 to restore, promote and celebrate traditional orchards became a charitable trust in 2011.[196]

The Old Court Nurseries were established by Ernest Ballard north of Colwall Stone *c.*1905, where he specialised in developing and breeding new varieties of asters and other autumnal species of flowers. Ballard died in 1952, and his former assistant Percy Picton purchased the nursery in 1956. The business remains in the same family in 2019.[197]

Mills

There was a mill on the bishop's manor in 1086, valued at 16*d.*[198] No demesne mill was recorded in the rental of *c.*1288, however, so the Domesday mill had probably already been alienated. It was presumably the mill then held by Geoffrey de Cradley by military service.[199] In 1578 the bishop's mill adjoined the park, and may have been the mill then called Colwall Farm held by Thomas Hill.[200] A map of 1806 marked the site of the former bishop's mill to the north of Lodge farm,[201] and it was recorded as a series of earthworks in 1887.[202] The former mill leet was adapted into a large fish pond during the 20th century.[203] Colwall mill stood on the Cradley Brook, near the boundary with Cradley and Mathon. One of these mills was presumably that held by John and Anne Hartland *c.*1612,[204] and the other by Leonard and Dorothy Pitt *c.*1605.[205] The mill held by the Hartlands, described as decayed by 1655, was held as part of the Hoars estate.[206]

William Holder held a little mill with his copyhold messuage called Lugg's in 1578,[207] held by Thomas Holder at the end of the century.[208] The mill later known as the Upper mill stood on Mill lane, between Colwall Green and the parish church, and was powered

193 HAS, AW86/2, p. 55.
194 Colwall Orchard Group Oral History.
195 *ODNB*, s.v. Knight, Thomas Andrew, horticulturist and plant physiologist (accessed 30 Sept. 2019).
196 Colwall Orchard Group, http://colwallorchardgroup.org/new%20home/index.html (accessed 9 May 2017); Char. Com. no. 1142573.
197 *Colwall Clock*, Jan. 2007; *Old Court Nurseries*, http://www.autumnasters.co.uk (accessed 9 June 2019).
198 *Domesday*, 502.
199 HAS, AA59/A/1, pp. 161, 167.
200 HAS, AA59/A/2 f. 63v.
201 BA, 31965[STG]/97.
202 OS Map, 25" (1888 edn), Herefs. XXXVI.5.
203 OS Map, 1:10000 (1974 edn), SO74SW.
204 TNA, CP/25/301/9JASIHIL.
205 TNA, CP/25/300/2JASIHIL.
206 HAS, D96/11.
207 HAS, AA59/A/2, f. 72v.
208 HAS, HD2/1/27; 9/3/77, will of James Brooke, 1598.

by the Chevenham brook.[209] It was in the possession of the Hartland family by 1530, when John Hartland conveyed it to his son, also John.[210] In 1578 Richard Hartland paid 6*d*. a year to the bishop for the use of the leet.[211] The mill was held by Richard and Joan Hartland *c*.1608,[212] who sold it in 1637 to William Brydges of Upleadon, who sold it in turn to Robert Bright in 1640.[213]

In the early 18th century, one of the mills was owned by Bridstock Harford and his sister Mary Jones.[214] It was still held by the Jones family in 1764, when Lugg's Mill was held by Henry Willis, and the remaining mill by Caleb Morton, the latter perhaps a tenant.[215] Colwall Mill farm was advertised for sale in 1790,[216] and was acquired by Lowbridge Bright.[217] By this date the mill had become redundant, and a map of 1806 marks its former location, and what remained of its leet, south of Colwall Mill farm.[218]

Both Lugg's and Upper Colwall Mills continued to function until the early 20th century. Lugg's was still occupied by the Willis family in 1853, while Upper Colwall Mill, owned by the Bright family, was occupied by James Kendrick in 1840, and by Thomas Baylis in 1853.[219] Elizabeth Mary Clee, wife of Alfred Clee, was admitted as tenant to Lugg's Mill in the early 20th century.[220] Lugg's Mill was disused by 1910; the mill pond at Upper Colwall Mill was filled in after the Second World War.[221]

By the late 13th century there was a windmill on 'le Pathull' on the Barton Colwall estate, granted by the dean and chapter to Robert of Colwall, vicar of Bishop's Frome, who conveyed it to John de Kempsey, later prebendary of Barton Colwall, in 1291.[222] The dean and chapter granted further leases of the mill in 1324 and 1346,[223] and it subsequently gave its name to the field in which it stood. It was referred to in 1608,[224] and again in 1681.[225] It stood on the high ground called the Windmill tump,[226] at or near Chance's Pitch.[227]

Industry and Crafts

The personal names of 13th- and 14th-century inhabitants included those derived from the trades of mason, smith, and tailor.[228] The weaver Richard Hooper, who made his

209 BA, 31965[STG]/97.
210 HAS, AA30/473.
211 HAS, AA59/A/2, f. 63v.
212 TNA, CP 25/2/300/6JASIMICH.
213 HAS, AA30/473, 476–8.
214 TNA, CP 25/2/929/10ANNEEASTER.
215 HAS, AE30/423.
216 *Heref. Jnl,* 14 Apr. 1790.
217 HAS, AA26/III/1; AA30/479–90.
218 BA, 31965[STG]/97.
219 HAS, AA26/III/2–3.
220 HAS, AA63/37, pp. 464–6.
221 OS Maps, 6" (1948 edn), Worcs. XLVI.NE; 1:10000 (1974 edn), SO74SW; Ballard, *Colwall Collection,* 87
222 DCA 354; 2050; TNA, CP 25/1/81/22 (133).
223 DCA 360, 1908
224 HAS, AE30/364–5.
225 HAS, AE30/88.
226 HAS, AA26/III/25.
227 HAS, AA26/III/1.
228 DCA 355; HAS, AA26/II/1, 10; AA59/A/1, pp. 163–4.

will in 1545, bequeathed his three looms and the other tools of his trade to his brother Thomas and one James Benson, and also referred to his apprentice, John Taylor.[229] Other weavers included Thomas Read in the late 16th century,[230] and Richard and Thomas Ockley in the mid 17th century.[231] Members of the Hartland, Pitt and Turner families were employed as butchers, tanners, glovers and tailors between the 16th and 18th centuries.[232] Brook house, also called Channam End and later known as the Tan house, was occupied in 1606 by the tanner Richard Hartland.[233] It was held by John Pitt, also a tanner, in 1650,[234] but during the 18th century was occupied by three generations of tanners called Richard Hartland, subsequently passing to a cousin, Philip Price (d. 1791), also a tanner.[235] John Daniel (d. 1677) was a shoemaker (corvisor),[236] as were two generations of the Hussey family. Robert the elder's inventory included leather, hemp, yarn and linen as well as his tools of trade and other tools.[237] His sons John (d. 1686) and Robert (d. 1732) followed him into the trade.[238] Other craftsmen in the parish in the late 17th and 18th centuries included a carpenter,[239] two coopers,[240] a glazier,[241] and two masons (one of whom also may have been a cooper).[242]

Of the 237 men aged 20 or above in 1831, 41 (17 per cent) were employed in retail and handicrafts, and one more in manufacturing.[243] By 1881 the number employed in industry and craft had risen to 93, including two women.[244] Reflecting the growth of the village after the arrival of the railway, 46 individuals were employed in the building trade, predominantly as carpenters or bricklayers. The railway employed another 16 men, and there were eight metal workers, seven ropemakers, five shoemakers, three tailors, and a female painter of china. Other crafts included two wheelwrights, a cooper, and a thatcher. By 1941 there had been a significant contraction in the numbers of craftsmen, when two carpenters, a blacksmith, and a cabinet-maker were in business in the parish.[245]

The Royal Malvern Well Brewery, or Royal Well Brewery, was established adjacent to the Royal Malvern Spa by 1879 by Arthur Bennett, who had the exclusive right from Ryland to brew with water from St Thomas' Well.[246] The business was acquired in 1884 by J. H. Tyler;[247] at his death in 1897, when the business was sold, the brewery was producing 4,000 barrels a year. Adjoining the brewery was a large residence, containing in 1897 five bedrooms.[248] The business changed hands twice between 1900, when it had

229 HAS, 23/1/3, will of Richard Hooper 1545.
230 HAS, 35/4/33, will of Thomas Read, 1590.
231 HAS, AE30/230, 240.
232 HAS, A72/2; AA26/II/44, 58; AE30/125–6, 237–40; TNA, PROB 11/335/333.
233 HAS, AE30/237.
234 HAS, AE30/229.
235 HAS, AE30/238–40.
236 HAS, 57/1/7, inventory of John Daniel 1677.
237 HAS, X2/5/13, will of Robert Hussie, 1684.
238 HAS, X2/5/12, will of John Hussie, 1686; TNA, PROB 11/652/321.
239 HAS, AE30/233; 92/1/4, will of Richard Ockley, 1685.
240 HAS, X2/5/22, inventory of Richard Cox, 1670; 83/1/16, inventory of Richard Mason, 1683; AE30/127.
241 HAS, AE30/481.
242 HAS, 83/1/16, inventory of Richard Mason, 1683; AE30/240.
243 Census, 1831.
244 Census, 1881.
245 *Kelly's Dir.* (1941 edn).
246 *Worc. Jnl,* 25 Oct. 1879.
247 *Worcs. Chronicle,* 6 Dec. 1884; 2 Jun. 1894.
248 *The Standard,* 29 Sep. 1897.

14 licensed premises, and 1903.[249] The company went into administration c.1931,[250] after which the brewery ceased to operate. Fred Ballard established a brick and tile works in Longlands field c.1890,[251] specialising in the blue bricks which can still be seen in buildings of the parish,[252] but it closed c.1903.[253] In 1897–8 Stephen Ballard, hoping to profit from the established trade in mineral water, established the Malvern Water Pure Ice Co. A building was constructed close to Grovesend Farm, where a well was sunk to extract cooling water, and an ice machine was ordered from the German company Linde at a cost of £1,600.[254] Ice was packed in hundredweight boxes and delivered by rail. The ice works later became a branch of the Worcester and Midlands Ice and Cold Storage Company, closing during the 1920s.[255]

Located on the fringe of Malvern, Upper Colwall proved attractive to businesses with interests on both sides of the Malvern Hills. William James established himself as a builder and contractor in Upper Colwall in 1889, with a large builders' yard behind his family home in Fossil Bank.[256] The firm undertook extensive work in Colwall, especially at the Schweppes mineral water factory, where William's father-in-law was appointed the foreman when it opened in 1892. James first worked for Schweppes in 1897, when he was responsible for the extension of the factory,[257] and his firm would be the preferred building contractors of Schweppes in the parish for the next 70 years.[258] Following William's death in 1921 the firm passed to his son Roland while Roland's brother Albert established himself as an electrical contractor. The company's peak was in the years following the Second World War, when it employed c.100 men.[259] The firm laid the main sewer pipe in the parish between 1934 and 1938, erected the Colwall clock and the public library, and built council houses in Orlin Road.[260] Work for Schweppes at its main factory included constructing new syrup rooms, building new warehouses, laying a new supply pipe to the factory from the Pewtress well, and constructing waste treatment works.[261] The firm also undertook commissions by institutions and individuals outside the parish, in particular in the Malvern area, building numerous houses, erecting the Friends' Meeting House in Orchard Road, and carrying out repairs and extensions to local schools and churches in Herefordshire and Worcestershire.[262] When the firm ceased trading in 1977, it had 37 employees on its books.[263]

In 1952 Roland James and William Bailey, a builders' merchant from Worcester, acquired the former brewery and mineral water works on West Malvern Road from

249 *Worcs. Chronicle*, 14 July 1900; 21 Dec. 1901; 9 May 1903; *Glos. Echo*, 25 July 1900.
250 *Daily Herald*, 11 Aug. 1931; T.B.V. Marsh, *The Commercial Complex (Now Residential) On West Malvern Road*, CVS (2002), 8.
251 HAS, AW86/2; E. Davey and R. Roseff, *Herefs. Bricks & Brickmakers* (Little Logaston, 2006), 83.
252 Above, Colwall Parish.
253 HAS, AW86/2; Ballard, *Colwall Collection*, 54–5.
254 Inf. from Linde Corporate Heritage, Linde AG.
255 HAS, AW98.
256 B.A. Sealey, *W. James Builders and Contractors 1889–1977*, CVS (2002).
257 HER, 31915; below, Malvern Water.
258 WAAS, 705:876 BA8077, 48.
259 Sealey, *W. James Builders and Contractors*
260 WAAS, 705:876 BA8077, 26–7.
261 WAAS, 705:876 BA8077, 47–9, 51–3.
262 WAAS, 705:876 BA8077, *passim*.
263 Sealey, *W. James Builders and Contractors*.

Schweppes. The premises, and Bailey's business, were subsequently purchased by the Walpamur paint and wallpaper company.[264] Walpamur used part of the site as a store for their builders' merchants businesses, while Bailey established the Wyche Tile and Fireplace Company on another part of the site.[265] After Walpamur ceased trading in 1966, Bailey purchased part of the property and continued trading under the name Wyche Fireplaces, while a chemical purification business was also established at the site.[266] The buildings were subsequently converted for residential use. An electrical engineering firm called Skot Transformers, originally founded at Hanley Swan (Worcs.) in 1963,[267] had moved its headquarters to Upper Colwall by 1986.[268] At its height, the company employed 88 people, divided between Upper Colwall and its factory at Malvern Link (Worcs.), but by the time the company folded in 2010 the number of employees had declined to 45.[269] Since 2012 the building has provided serviced office-space and industrial units for local businesses.[270]

Quarrying

A deed of 1608 referred to a quarry pit in Windmill field,[271] presumably one of several old quarries recorded near Chance's Pitch c.1886.[272] The western slopes of the Malvern Hills comprised a band of limestone,[273] which by the 18th century was burned to produce large quantities of lime for agricultural uses.[274] The tenants of Brockbury were keen in 1781 for permission to be granted for a new limekiln on the manor to improve husbandry,[275] and a map of 1806 recorded the location of several lime kilns in the east of the parish.[276] Lime was also used in the tanning process, and Brook House farm was said in 1800 to be very close to an extensive lime works.[277] A man was employed as a lime burner and mason in 1784,[278] and two men were occupied as lime burners in 1841.[279]

Numerous abandoned quarries and lime kilns were recorded on the western slopes of the Malvern Hills c.1886, particularly east and south of Evendine, and to the north and west of Upper Colwall.[280] Many quarries were still being worked within Colwall common,

264 Marsh, *Commercial Complex On West Malvern Road*, 8.

265 Ibid., 8–9; *Tewkesbury Register*, 12 Jun. 1964.

266 Marsh, *Commercial Complex On West Malvern Road*, 8–9.

267 *Malvern Gaz.*, 10 Feb. 2010.

268 HAS, CG3/6, p. 284.

269 *Worcester News*, 9 Jan. 2010.

270 *Colwall Clock*, Mar. 2012; https://www.wyche-innovation.com (accessed 21 May 2019).

271 HAS, AE30/364–5.

272 OS Map, 25" (1888 edn), Herefs. XXXVI.10.

273 Above, Colwall Parish.

274 J. Barrett, [*A Description of Malvern and Its Environs*] (Worc. 1796), 22; J. Clark, *A General View of the Agriculture of the County of Heref.* (1794), 23–4; J. Duncumb, *A General View of the Agriculture of the County of Heref.* (1802), 103–5.

275 HAS, AE30/81a.

276 BA, 31965[STG]/97.

277 *Heref. Jnl*, 5 Feb. 1800.

278 Eastnor Castle Archive, Colwall Deeds, indenture of 21 Dec. 1784.

279 Census, 1841.

280 OS Map, 25" (1888 edn), Herefs. XXXVI.2–3, 6, 10; HER, 21123; 21169; 21170; 40386; 40388–408; 40418–9; 40423–7.

in particular to supply stone for the building of roads.[281] Although the Malvern Hills Act of 1884 did not prohibit quarrying, all but two of the quarries in Colwall, Gardiner's and the Wyche, were closed *c.*1886.[282] Despite this, the conservators could not prevent the Ledbury highway board opening a new quarry near the Wyche in 1888.[283] In 1924 powers were given to Minister of Agriculture and to the conservators to prevent quarrying in the hills,[284] and a ministerial decision was made in 1953 that ultimately all quarrying on the Malvern Hills should cease. However, this would be a gradual process to reduce the impact on the economy and employment.[285]

Malvern Water

Schweppes began bottling water at the Holy Well in Malvern Wells (Worcs.) in 1850, successfully marketing it as Malvern Soda at the Great Exhibition in the following year.[286] A new bottling plant opened near Colwall railway station in 1892, initially employing 17 people,[287] drawing water from the Glenwood spring at Winnings Farm.[288] An attempt to bore a well at the factory site was abandoned when it produced salt water. The plant, which drew praise from *The Builder* for the way in which it harmonised with its setting, took the form of an H-shaped complex, one wing of which was lengthened *c.*1897.[289] The bottled water was drawn from the Glenwood spring until 1928, when a long lease was signed for the use of water from the Pewtress spring (now called Primeswell) on the western side of the Herefordshire Beacon.[290] The plant was expanded before 1946, perhaps during the Second World War, when production had to be moved from factories in London and Bristol. By 1956 the company employed 140 people in the parish, but this fell to 25 by the mid 1990s.[291] Production continued at the main Colwall Schweppes plant until its closure in 2010,[292] after which it was demolished.

The Royal Wells Mineral Water Works, a separate venture on the parish boundary with West Malvern was established before the end of the 19th century. The company was acquired by Allen Bros. *c.* 1901, and was subsequently acquired by Berkeley and Co. Mineral Water, which continued to bottle water at the site until the 1940s.[293] The Royal Wells water works was also owned by Schweppes by 1945,[294] but was sold in 1952.[295]

Broadwood Park, adjacent to Winnings Farm, was acquired for warehousing and distribution, but was adapted for use as a production plant during the Second World War, when the Kia-Ora soft drinks company, a Schweppes subsidiary, was evacuated

281 HAS, K41/2, pp. 332, 345.
282 MHC minute book, 1884–6, pp. 127, 141. Below, Local Government.
283 MHC minute book, 1888–9, p. 46.
284 14 & 15 Geo. V c.xxxvi.
285 Hurle, *Forest and Chase*, 133–4.
286 *PastScape*, no. 1534167; D.A. Simmons, *Schweppes: the first 200 years* (1983), 48.
287 J. Hall, *A Brief History of the Colwall Schweppes Factory*, CVS, C21.
288 Above, Colwall Parish.
289 *The Builder*, 30 Jan. 1892, 80; HAS, CP 59 6/6.
290 L. Richardson, *Memoirs of the Geological Survey, England: Wells and Springs of Herefs.* (1935), 72.
291 Hall, *Colwall Schweppes Factory*.
292 *Daily Telegraph*, 21 Oct. 2010; HAS, CP 59 6/6.
293 WAAS, 705:876 BA8077 47; Marsh, *The Commercial Complex On West Malvern Road*, 8.
294 HAS, BW15/13/2, 24 Sept. 1845; WAAS, 705:876 BA 8077 48, 50.
295 WAAS, 705:876 BA8077 47.

there from London.[296] It reverted to Schweppes after the war, and was closed in 1962. By 1970 the site was operated by Tesco supermarkets as a packing station,[297] but was disused by 1986, by which time it was called Snatford.[298]

Vinegar Brewery

Stephen Ballard purchased a vinegar brewery in Ledbury in 1883, and production was moved to Colwall the following year, to take advantage of spring water on Ballard's estate.[299] The new plant comprised a barley store, grinding mills and fermentation vats, and at its peak it was producing 2,000 gallons of vinegar a day.[300] A sawmill was constructed to build crates for packing the bottles,[301] which were then transported to Colwall railway station for distribution. The business was well integrated with other parts of the Ballard's estates. Pickles were produced to help sell the vinegar, and soft fruit was also bottled at the plant.[302] The waste barley from the brewing process was transported by a short tramway to feed pigs at the Ballard piggery.[303] Although the malt vinegar was well regarded, winning prizes in Paris (1889) and Edinburgh (1890), the company was not profitable, and was sold to Fardon's of Birmingham in 1914, when production ceased at Colwall.[304] The factory was subsequently used for canning fruit until 1961, after which it was used as a plastic toy factory, and was demolished in 1992.[305]

Distributive and Service Trades

By 1851 there were nine shops in the parish: four at Colwall Green, two at Upper Colwall, and one each at Evendine, Walwyn Road and Old Church Road.[306] During the last years of the 19th century rows of shop-fronted houses were built on Walwyn Road,[307] and by 1922 there were 17 shops in the parish.[308] In 1941 shopkeepers in the parish included four grocers, three butchers, a dairyman, a hairdresser, a newsagent, and two china and glass dealers.[309] The number of stores reached a maximum of 22 by the mid 20th century, substantially more than neighbouring villages such as Bosbury and Eastnor.[310] By 1950 there were shops belonging to three butchers, a baker, a confectioner (also the post office), a grocer, a fruiterer, a chemist, a newsagent, an ironmonger, a wool dealer, and a hairdresser.[311] The rapid increase in car ownership and the opening

---

296 WAAS, 705:876 BA8077 48, 53.
297 HAS, BW15/13/10, 1/6/1971.
298 HAS, CG36/3, pp. 239, 259; WAAS, 592:01 BA14605, 24 Nov. 1989.
299 HAS, AW98.
300 HAS, AW98.
301 Ballard, *Colwall Collection*, 24–6.
302 HAS, AW98.
303 HAS, K13/20; AW86/2, p. 28.
304 B. Osborne and C. Weaver, *Celebrated Springs of the Malvern Hills* (Andover, 2012), 62–3; Ballard, *Colwall Collection*, 20–3; Hurle, *Ballard*, 84.
305 HAS, AW98; CG36/9, 27 Apr. 1992.
306 *Lascelles Dir.* (1851 edn).
307 Above, Colwall Parish.
308 *Littlebury's Dir.* (1867, 1876 edns); *Kelly's Dir.* (1885–1937 edns).
309 *Kelly's Dir.* (1941 edn).
310 *VCH Herefs.*, Bosbury, 49; Eastnor, 57.
311 *Kelly's Dir. of Great Malvern* (1950 edn).

Figure 18 *Aerial photograph of the former malt vinegar works in 1933 when being used for fruit canning.*

of supermarkets in Malvern and Ledbury led to a decline after the 1970s. In 2019 only seven shops remain. An agency of the Capital and Counties bank opened in Colwall in 1896, but became part of Lloyds Bank in 1918, and closed in 1993.[312] A second bank was opened by the Midland Bank on Station Road in 1923, which closed at the end of the 20th century.[313]

John Meates of Barton Farm established himself as a coal merchant in the second half of the 19th century, with depots at Colwall railway station and Ledbury, and later at Ashperton canal wharf, Stoke Edith and Newent.[314] His children carried on the business until after the Second World War.[315] By 1895 Thomas Wilkins of Barton Court farm had a business dealing in agricultural implements and artificial manure.[316] By 1901 he had moved to Chance's Pitch and was also acting as an agricultural and electrical engineer.[317] Two garages were established in the early 20th century, one opposite Colwall Park Hotel

312 Inf. provided by Peter Judge, Archivist, Lloyds Banking Group.
313 Inf. provided by HSBC Archives.
314 *PO Dir.* (1863 edn); *Littlebury's Dir.* (1876/7 edn).
315 TNA, RG 12/2051; *Kelly's Dir.* (1922, 1934, 1941 edns).
316 *PO Dir.* (1879 edn); *Kelly's Dir.* (1895 edn).
317 TNA, RG 13/2470, RG 14/15605–6; *Kelly's Dir.* (1909, 1913, 1917 edns).

Figure 19 *Ballard's Malt Vinegar label.*

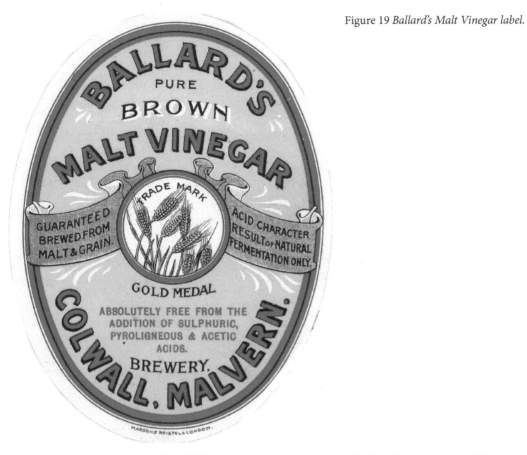

and the other at Upper Colwall.[318] A petrol pump was installed at the garage in Upper Colwall in 1953,[319] and there was a petrol station at Chance's pitch by 1957.[320] All three garages closed between 1980 and 1989.[321]

Leisure and Tourism

The springs rising on both sides of the Malvern Hills were known for their healing qualities by the 17th century.[322] The 1633 map of Malvern Chase marks St. Thomas's Well and Moorarls' Well within Colwall common,[323] and a brick-lined bath and wash pool had been established at the latter by 1806.[324] It was disused in 1817, although its

---

318   MHC minute book, 1931–5, p. 234; HAS, BW15/13/2, 9 Apr. 1940.

319   MHC minute book, 1947–54, p. 157.

320   HAS, BW15/13/4, p. 313.

321   WAAS, 592:01 BA14605 26, 27 Mar. 1980; 30/1, 12 Nov. 1988; HAS, CG36/3, p. 525.

322   Smith, Malvern, 171–3; J. Beale, 'An account of some sanative-waters in Herefs.' *Phil. Trans. Royal Soc.* 1 (1665–6), 358–9.

323   WAAS, X705:24 BA81/366; C. Weaver and B. Osborne, *Aquae Malvernensis: the springs and fountains of the Malvern Hills* (Malvern, 1994), 54, 68.

324   BA, 31965[STG]/97.

reputation for the treatment of eyes was still recorded in the 1880s.[325] Another well close
to the Wyche cutting, marked in 1806 by the name Prims Well but later known as Willow
Spring, was used by patients walking or taking a donkey up from Great Malvern.[326]

The water of St Thomas' Well, on the boundary of the parish with West Malvern,
was promoted from the 1870s by William Hawker Ryland, who acquired the spring and
surrounding land after taking the water whilst recuperating. He opened a public spout
in 1870, and subsequently constructed a large spa with hall, baths, an art gallery and
pleasure grounds, which opened in 1883 with a performance by Jenny Lind.[327] Despite
this, the spa was unable to compete with the attractions of Malvern, where the Assembly
Rooms opened two years later. The spa closed in 1895,[328] and the buildings were
demolished c.1937.[329] The Rylands Royal Well spout remains in public use in 2019.[330]

The Malvern Hills have been a focal point for travellers for centuries, and the
Herefordshire Beacon may be the summit from which John Evelyn described seeing as
far as Derbyshire.[331] In modern times, British Camp has proved alluring to those enjoying
the nearby facilities of Great Malvern and for day-trippers from further afield. Between
April and September 1939, British Camp was visited by almost 500 special coach trips,
while more than 1,600 regular bus services stopped there during the same period.[332] The
hill fort remains a popular attraction in 2019, with a large proportion of the Malvern
Hills' annual 1.25 million visitors visiting Colwall.[333]

A house at Wind's Point (now known as Wynd's Point) was marked on a map of 1832,
called the Wind's Point inn by 1846,[334] and the British Camp inn by 1853.[335] Besides
providing refreshment to travellers climbing the main road between Ledbury and Little
Malvern, it was a regular venue for annual summer picnics and other parties in the
middle of the 19th century.[336] In 1919 it comprised a public lounge and bar, sitting room,
dining room, smoking room, and 12 bedrooms.[337] Besides providing accommodation
for travellers, the hotel also catered for individuals making excursions to see the British
Camp, providing a café and public toilet facilities.[338] Its name was changed to the Malvern
Hills Hotel in 1975.[339]

The first boarding house was listed in directories in 1863, soon after the arrival of
the railway.[340] There was still one lodging house in 1879, but by 1895 there were two and

325 N. May, *Guide to Malvern* (1882), 141 cited in Weaver and Osborne, *Aquae Malvernensis*, 69.
326 L. Richardson, *Memoirs of the Geological Survey, England: Wells and Springs of Herefs.* (1935), 71; *Aquae Malvernensis*, 64.
327 *Malvern Gaz.* 5 May 1883; below, Social History.
328 Smith, *Malvern*, 211.
329 OS Map, 6" (1948 edn), Worcs. XXXIX.SE.
330 http://www.malvernwaters.com/nationalparks.asp?search=yes&p=7&id=243 (accessed 1 Nov. 2019)
331 E.S. De Beer (ed), *The Diary of John Evelyn, ed. John Bowle* (Oxford, 1985), 161
332 MHC minute book, 1938–47, p. 51.
333 http://www.malvernhillsaonb.org.uk/about-the-aonb/key-features-malvern-hills-aonb (accessed 6 Oct. 2019).
334 *Heref. Times*, 10 Oct. 1846.
335 *Heref. Times*, 20 Aug. 1853; *PO Dir. of Herefs.* (1856 edn).
336 *Worcs. Chronicle* 26 July 1854; *Heref. Times*, 22 Aug. 1857; 14 Sept. 1861.
337 HAS, M5/6/70.
338 MHC minute book, 1966–9, pp. 63, 119–20; HAS, CG36/2; WAAS, 592:01 BA14605 25, 7 Mar. 1979.
339 *Malvern Hills Hotel*, http://malvernhillshotel.co.uk (accessed 18 Apr. 2017).
340 *PO Dir.* (1863 edn).

Figure 20 *Photograph of Colwall Park Hotel in 2019.*

another seven places offered 'apartments'. By 1922 twelve sets of apartments were listed.[341] Some were provided by retired tradespeople like Matthew Manton, a former shoemaker; others were offered by craftsmen's wives or spinsters, with boarding houses run by married ladies.[342] By the late 1930s more apartments were for rent and refreshment rooms opened for trade.[343]

The Colwall Park Hotel, built by Roland Cave-Brown-Cave of Barton Court, opened in 1907 on the site of Stone Farm, conveniently near the railway station. Following its builder's bankruptcy in 1909[344] the hotel was sold, the sales particulars of 1912 noting that Colwall was 'fast gaining popularity as a Holiday and Health Resort'.[345] In 1914 it offered suites of apartments and advertised 'every accommodation' for motorists and golfers, with loose boxes for hunters.[346] In the 1920s it advertised facilities for early motorists: a garage, petrol, oil, and cars for hire. By 1923 the owner J. Scott-Bowden had changed the name to the Park Hotel.[347] It remains a hotel in 2019.

341 *PO Dir.* (1879 edn); *Kelly's Dir.* (1895 edn).
342 *Kelly's Dir.* (1909, 1922, 1934, 1941 edns).
343 *Kelly's Dir.* (1937, 1941 edn).
344 *Glouc. Citizen*, 23 Dec. 1909; *Glouc. Jnl*, 6 Aug. 1910.
345 HAS, M5/6/66.
346 *Jakeman and Carver's Dir. of Herefs.* (1914 edn).
347 Deeds of Stone Holt, Colwall, in private hands.

SOCIAL HISTORY

IN THE MIDDLE AGES THE bishop of Hereford and the prebendary of Barton Colwall were the major landowners but visited infrequently, while the lord of Brockbury was usually resident. Colwall was a community of small farmers and labourers. Between the 15th and 17th centuries resident gentry established themselves on other estates, playing an important part in the social life of the parish. In the 19th century the presence of prominent landowning families, in particular the Ballards, provided social leadership in the community. Colwall Stone became the focal point for communal activities. Walwyn's Free Grammar School was founded in 1614 and other schools were established in the 19th and early 20th centuries. The parish administered poor relief until 1834 when Colwall became part of Ledbury poor-law union. Several charities were endowed for the benefit of parishioners.

Social Character

The Middle Ages

A total of 77 tenants were recorded in the *c.*1288 survey, combining the bishop's two manors of Colwall and Coddington.[1] One holding, of four yardlands held as the sixth part of a knight's fee, belonged to a free tenant, Philip Ruddock, who paid no rent but owed suit of court, relief and scutage appropriate to a tenant by knight service. Another free tenant, Robert de Frome, with 76 a. of free land, was probably the precursor of the franklin who is identified in the poll tax of 1379.[2] Most of the numerous freeholders, of whom 43 were listed *c.*1288, had very modest quantities of land, and 20 of them, 47 per cent of the total, can be classified as smallholders with 6 a. or less. The privileged status of freedom contrasted with their limited landed resources. The 34 customary tenants tended to have larger holdings, with only nine smallholders. Twenty-three customary tenants (59 per cent) held 15 a. or more, compared with 47 per cent of freeholders. All of the customary tenants owed the bishop a 'gift', sometimes also with honey and fish, and 21 of them were expected to supply one or two geese. These payments in kind are likely to have been survivals from a much earlier period. The customary tenants with fractions of a yardland had once owed labour services, but these had been converted by the late 13th century into money rents of 13*s.* ½*d.* for a half-yardland, or a modest 5*d.* per acre. The ability of Colwall tenants to pay rents in cash supposes that they sold produce to raise the money, and no doubt gained a surplus to spend for themselves. The market at Ledbury must have been very familiar to them. The lowest status tenants were perhaps the 11 *operaciones* (workers) who mostly held 3 a. or 6 a., though two had 12 a.

---

1   HAS, AA59/A/1, pp. 160–7.
2   *Poll Taxes 1377–81*, ed. Fenwick, pt 1, 371.

They were all expected to work for one or two days each week throughout the year, and one was required to drive animals 'from place to place', or to carry hens and geese when needed. These underprivileged tenants may have been descended from the slaves of the 11th century. The free and customary tenants were not rigidly divided, as 14 of the customary tenants held free land, mostly in quite small parcels. The main function of the tenants from the point of view of the lord of the manor was to pay rent, and work on the demesne, but tenants included specialists such as the hawker and two parkers who maintained the bishops' hunting facilities, and the beadle who performed administrative duties.

Despite the archaic survivals implied by rents and services, the population of Colwall, like most villages of the period, was by no means unchanging. Surnames such as Cradley and Stow *c.*1288 show that some families originated outside the parish, and presumed emigrants called Colwall are recorded in Worcestershire around 1300. In the 1440s and 1450s, two resident Frenchmen contributed to the 'alien subsidy', called Perinus Hawthorne and Janyn Frenschmon, though the latter possibly held land elsewhere in Herefordshire, including Ledbury and Eastnor.[3]

Although the bishops were necessarily absentee lords, they appear to have visited the manor regularly during the 13th century, in part drawn by their hunting grounds there. Bishop Swinfield spent Easter 1290 and the week afterwards, ten days in total, at Colwall, where the large number of horses in the stables indicate he was joined by many guests. The manor was poorly-provisioned, perhaps because produce from the manor was taken to Bosbury, which acted as a local store for the bishop's manors, and much of the food and drink for the feasting had to be brought from elsewhere.[4] Two lean deer from the chase were also provided for the bishop's table during his stay. The bishop returned to Colwall again in July, in order to hunt in the chase.[5]

In 1334 Colwall and Coddington together were taxed at a similar level as their neighbour Cradley, but paid almost twice as much as Bosbury.[6] In 1377 there were 133 men aged 14 or over in Colwall and Coddington, more populous than Bosbury, with 92, but fewer than Cradley, with 186.[7] The names of 36 inhabitants of Colwall were recorded in 1379, along with eight unnamed entries, and part of the membrane is faded. Most of those recorded on this damaged roll paid an assessment of 4*d.*, but one John Farne was taxed at 3*s.* 4*d.*, and two others were taxed at 12*d.* and 6*d.* respectively.[8]

16th to 18th Centuries

In 1524, a total of 34 people were assessed for the subsidy in Colwall, divided almost equally between the two tithings of Barton and Colwall, one on a customary holding, four on wages and the rest on goods.[9] In Colwall, John Hartland was assessed on goods worth 20 marks (£13 6*s.* 8*d.*), twice that of the next highest assessment of £6 13*s.* 4*d.* of

3 https://www.englandsimmigrants.com, nos 56803, 57291, 57517, 57581, 57620, 58578, 58587 (accessed 23 Oct. 2019)
4 *Expenses of Swinfield*, LXII, clxvi–clxvii.
5 *Expenses of Swinfield*, LXII, ccxxxii.
6 *The Lay Subsidy Roll of 1334*, ed. R.E. Glasscock (1975), 129.
7 *Poll Taxes 1377–81*, ed. Fenwick, pt 1, 358.
8 *Poll Taxes 1377–81*, ed. Fenwick, pt 1, 371–2.
9 *Herefs. Taxes*, 63–4.

William Ockley.[10] Members of the Hartland family held the Hoar,[11] Cummins farm,[12] and Colwall mill.[13] Seven other individuals were assessed at values between £3 and £6, including one member each of the Ockley and Hartland families, two members of the Broke family, and one widow, Perina Hope, who named John Hartland as her executor in 1530.[14] John Hill held a large enough holding of customary land to be assessed at 20s. for it. In Barton, John Pitt was assessed for £18 worth of goods.[15] He or a namesake held land belonging to the priory of Little Malvern during the 16th century, perhaps the tenement called Deanhaule,[16] and the widow Anne Pitt was described in 1608 as of Oldcastle.[17] Five other inhabitants of Barton were assessed at £3 each in 1524, including one widow.

Twenty years later, 49 individuals, including six widows, were assessed on goods worth between £1 and £9.[18] After John Hartland, at £9, Richard Gylding was assessed at £8 and Katherine Broke at £7. Five members of the Pitt family were assessed on a combined total of goods worth £21, closely followed by three members of the Gylding family, who together were assessed on goods of £19. In total, 15 individuals were assessed on goods worth £5 or more, and 34 on goods worth £4 or less. A late-16th-century survey found that eight of the 37 freehold and customary tenements on the bishop's manor were 'unbuilt', perhaps the result of late medieval depopulation. The manor was let to the bishop's son, Silvan Scory, who was not resident. The survey listed 18 freehold and 16 customary tenements, although three of the latter were held by freeholders.[19] The freeholders included John Walwyn, owner of Brockbury with four yardlands of land, and Robert Hartland, who held three yardlands including the estate called Hoars.[20] Of the customary tenements, Richard Gylding's lands at Old Colwall amounted to c.86 a., and William Hill held an estate of c.55 a., while three men held fewer than 10 a.[21]

Unsurprisingly, with the two principal manors of the parish held by absentee ecclesiastics, few individuals within the parish were considered gentlemen during the early modern period. In the 16th and early 17th century the tenants of the ecclesiastical estates were often also gentlemen, who sublet the estates in parcels to prospering families within the parish. The Berkeleys – Thomas and his son Maurice, both accounted gentlemen – leased the prebendal estate in the late 17th century.[22] The owners of Brockbury – the Cowleys, the Walwyns and the Brights – were always described as gentlemen. In the late 17th century the Pitts of Oldcastle and the Pritchards of Hope End were also called gentlemen.

10   *Herefs. Taxes,* 64.
11   Above, Landownership.
12   HAS, AE30/468–72.
13   HAS, AE30/473.
14   *Cal. of Probate and Administration Acts in the Court Books of the Bishops of Hereford 1407–1541,* ed. M.A. Faraday and E.J.L. Cole (1989), 257.
15   *Herefs. Taxes, 63.*
16   *Cal. Pat.* 1553–4, 457; HAS, A72/2–3; AE30/346.
17   *Cal. Pat.* 1553–4, 337; HAS, AE30/346.
18   *Herefs. Taxes, 310.*
19   HAS, AA59/A/2, ff. 62v–66v.
20   HAS, AA58/A/2, f. 63.
21   HAS, AA58/A/2, ff. 69v–80.
22   TNA, PROB 4/6575; PROB 11/306/176.

Surviving probate inventories of the 16th and 17th centuries reveal few had any luxury items beyond feather mattresses and pillows: one woman owned three silver cups, one man owned four gilded leather chairs.[23] Only four testators bequeathed any books.[24] Instead, surplus wealth was reinvested by the prosperous families of Colwall into land and livestock. The appraisers of the estate of William Brook of the Brookhouse valued it at over £157 when he died, yet he still ate from wooden and earthenware crockery, while his livestock and his plough tack accounted for c.£79 of the total, and crops, wool, and his plough gear another £44.[25] Even the gentleman Rowland Pitt had few valuable personal items in his estate, worth £204 at his death, of which livestock and tack comprised £86, crops another £57 (including £34 in money owed to him for hops), and timber £13.[26] John Nelme had a substantial sum of cash in his possession at his death, his clothes and the money in his purse together worth £141 of the total sum of £318, of which debts owed to him amounted for another £84 10s. Of the remaining estate, livestock and tack accounted for £50, and crops £14.[27]

Taxation records of the late 17th century reveal the increased disparity of wealth. Three parishioners – Bridstock Harford (a medical doctor who probably resided at Hereford),[28] Robert Bright and Maurice Berkeley – were assessed at £70 or more in 1663 for the maintenance of the militia, more than double the next highest assessments. Seven other estates were valued between £20 and £35. The remaining 51 taxpayers were assessed below this level, many for sums of between £2 and £3.[29] The hearth tax assessment of 1665 presents a similar picture. Of 66 householders charged with the tax, only 13 had three or more hearths, and only three – Henry Wright, Maurice Berkeley, and Richard Cox – had six or more.[30]

During the 18th century this small group of gentry families consolidated their position and estates.[31] A junior branch of the Brydges family of Upleadon (Herefs.) acquired an estate in Old Colwall in the late 17th century, and the Pritchards built up a large estate centred upon Hope End that crossed the parish boundaries. The resident gentry began to display their position more prominently through the building of elegant mansions, augmented at Brockbury and Hope End by carefully designed landscapes.[32] All five sons of Henry Bright (d. 1726) of Brockbury left the parish to set up in trade at Bristol, becoming prominent in the slave trade. His heir Robert (d. 1758) and another son both died in Jamaica.[33] Henry's second son, Henry (d. 1777), was a successful merchant, managing 21 slave voyages between 1749 and 1766, and serving as mayor of Bristol in 1771.[34] In the next generation, both Lowbridge and Richard Bright were

23   HAS, 29/2/31 inventory of John Barston, 1670; X2/5/20, inventory of Mary Hall, 1676.
24   HAS, 14/3/23 inventory of Milborough Watt, 1610; X2/5/3 will of Blanche Hartland of Evendine 1665; 29/2/31 inventory of John Barston, 1670; 44/2/21 inventory of William Hill, 1675.
25   HAS, X2/5/6 inventory of William Brook 1661.
26   HAS, 94/1/30 inventory of Rowland Pitt 1686.
27   HAS, 126/6/10 inventory of John Nelme 1697.
28   *Hist. Parl.* 1660–90, 492–3.
29   *Herefs. Militia Assessments*, 94.
30   HAS, AM29/1, 70.
31   Above, Landownership.
32   Above, Colwall Parish.
33   *Herald & Genealogist*, VII, 503–11.
34   *ODNB*, s.v. Bright, Henry, merchant (accessed 30 Sept. 2019); above, Landownership.

successfully established in trade at Bristol, before each succeeded in turn to the manor of Brockbury. A younger son of Richard became established in trade at Liverpool during the 19th century. His son returned to Colwall to purchase Brockbury in the 20th century.[35]

Since 1800

Despite the mercantile background of the Brights, the banker James Martin, and the sugar planter Edward Moulton Barrett, Colwall was a place for professionals to settle into gentrified retirement, providing a quiet idyll for Barrett's daughter, the poet Elizabeth Barrett Browning, to publish her first poems.[36] Until the middle of the 19th century Colwall remained a largely agricultural community and legal, medical and financial services had to be sought at Ledbury or Malvern. In 1831 more than half of the 237 men aged 20 and over in Colwall were employed in agriculture, with 102 agricultural labourers employed by 16 farmers; six more farmers employed no labourers.[37] Forty-one men were employed in handicrafts or retail, and 33 as non-agricultural labourers. Six individuals were recorded as professionals, and there were just eight male servants. One individual was employed in manufacturing and 24 were occupied in some other way, probably mainly living by independent means.

The social structure and character of Colwall changed markedly in the later 19th century. The building of the railway line between Worcester and Hereford attracted a large number of labourers, tunnel diggers, and civil engineers to the parish for a time,[38] besides providing opportunities for industry in the parish.[39] These were exploited by the engineer and entrepreneur Stephen Ballard, who occupied the Winnings and had been instrumental in the building of the railway.[40] By 1881 just 98 of the parish's 376 men (26 per cent) were employed in agriculture.[41] Reflecting Colwall's growing reputation as a pleasant retreat, temporary or permanent, 46 men were employed in housebuilding or furnishings, 79 dealt in commodities, and 16 were employed in the hospitality trades. Quarrying was also important, with 24 men employed in the working or dealing of minerals. There were 12 professionals, three employed in commercial occupations, and 38 men employed in domestic service. The 1881 census also recorded the occupations of women, with 125 employed in service and 23 in textiles. Fourteen women were recorded as professionals, predominantly teachers, and three dealt in books and prints. Nevertheless, the proximity of Ledbury and Malvern meant that these towns provided specialist services for the district, and it was not until the beginning of the 20th century that offices opened in Colwall for solicitors, an architect and a surveyor.[42]

Colwall's particular beauty and its proximity to Malvern drew a small colony of artists and writers to the parish from the late 19th century. Colwall's attraction was preserved by the efforts of local gentlemen including Robert Raper and Stephen Ballard, who were

---

35   Above, Landownership.
36   *ODNB*, s.v. Browning [née Moulton Barrett], Elizabeth Barrett (accessed 9 Jan. 2020).
37   Census, 1831.
38   Census, 1861.
39   Above, Economic History.
40   Hurle, *Stephen Ballard*; *ODNB*, s.v. Ballard, Stephen, civil engineer (accessed 30 Sept. 2019); above, Economic History.
40   'Colwall Occupation data 1881', http://www.visionofbritain.org.uk/unit/10078271/cube/OCC_ ORDER1881 (accessed 8 Apr. 2019).
42   *Worcs. Chron.* 7 Sept. 1901; 28 Mar. 1903; *Glouc. Citizen*, 13 Aug. 1921.

instrumental in the passage of the Malvern Hills Act of 1884, which preserved the hills as a public space in their undeveloped state.[43] The most notable of Colwall's new residents was Jenny Lind (d. 1887), renowned as the 'Swedish Nightingale', a distinguished soprano who had toured extensively throughout Europe, North America and Cuba, before retiring to Colwall.[44] Her last performance was given at a charity concert at the Royal Malvern Spa Hall in 1883. The theatre director and entrepreneur Sir Barry Vincent Jackson, who founded the Birmingham Repertory Theatre in 1913, moved to Black Hill near British Camp in the late 1920s, establishing an annual festival celebrating George Bernard Shaw at Malvern.[45] The poet W. H. Auden was employed at the Downs school between 1933 and 1935, and the Canadian author Mazo de la Roche lived at the Winnings between 1935 and 1937.[46] The artists Harold (d. 1961) and Dame Laura Knight (d. 1970) spent much of the later years of their lives at Colwall.[47]

Communal Life

In 1588 William Poole was accused of allowing piping and tabouring in his house, at or called the Black Hill, presumably an inn.[48] A tract of c.1600 describes, with evident hostility, the Sunday recreations of the parishioners, centred upon the church house, a building erected near the church by the parish c.1531 for a range of functions, including the brewing and serving of ale at parish celebrations.[49] The anonymous godly author recounted that 'a Master of Misrule' entertained revellers 'with drums & Bagpipes & with warlike Gunnnes', which he likened to 'May games'. The parishioners left church 'Mid-service' to 'carouse' at the church house with their 'Priest', then returned to church for afternoon prayers, before feasting and dancing around a May pole for the rest of the day. It may have been a similar event which led to the presentation of Gabriel Pitt and six others in 1619, for dancing on Sunday between morning and evening prayer. Pitt unsuccessfully argued that his house in Barton Colwall was outside the jurisdiction of the court.[50]

The former church house was extended in the 17th century and converted into three cottages.[51] These housed the poor until 1848, when the new rector, Frederick Custance, proposed replacing them with two new cottages, one of which would be for the parish clerk. Although his proposal was not acted upon, the upper storey of the cottages may have been removed at that time. The building may also have ceased to house the poor, as parish meetings were regularly held there from 1851.[52] The building, known locally as the church ale house, was subsequently converted into a parish meeting hall in 1987. In 2019 it continues to be used as a venue for community activities.

43   Below, Local Government.
44   *ODNB*, s.v. Lind, Jenny, singer (accessed 30 Sept. 2019).
45   *ODNB*, s.v. Jackson, Sir Barry Vincent, theatre director (accessed 30 Sept. 2019).
46   M. De la Roche, *Ringing the Changes: an Autobiography* (1957), 253.
47   *ODNB*, s.v. Knight [née Johnson], Dame Laura, painter (accessed 30 Sept. 2019).
48   *Recs. of Early English Drama: Herefs. and Worcs.* ed. D.N. Klausner (1990), 69–70.
49   BL, Add. MS 14826, f. 96.
50   *Recs. of Early English Drama*, 70–2.
51   Below, Religious Life.
52   HAS, CK23/44, pp. 416, 435; *Heref. Jnl*, 28 Feb. 1849; *Littlebury's Dir.* (1876).

Figure 21 *Photograph of Colwall Church Cottage, the former church house on the perimeter of the churchyard.*

There appear to have been no friendly societies in Colwall until the late 19th century, but parishioners may have been members of the Ledbury Friendly Assurance Society, established in 1835 with support from the clergy and gentry of Colwall.[53] A benefit society was established in 1873 with 11 members and assets worth £10.[54] It was reported to meet in the British Camp inn in 1877, when its membership had fallen to eight but its collective assets had grown to £15.[55] The Loyal Perseverance Lodge of the Independent Order of Oddfellows, Manchester Union was established in 1876.[56] Meeting at the Horse & Groom inn, it had 28 members and assets worth £57. The benefit society based at British Camp inn had either folded or combined with the Odd Fellows by 1879, when the latter was the only society in the parish, with a membership of 48.[57] By 1887 the membership had grown to 68, of whom 11 had joined in the previous year.[58] In 1911 the membership numbered 201, and the lodge's total assets amounted to £2,065.[59] A women's branch of the Oddfellows, the Loyal Bright Female Lodge, was established in 1902 at the Workmen's Hall, and by 1911 it had 64 members.[60]

Stephen Ballard, at the centre of so much of parish life in the second half of the 19th century, played an important role in the communal life of the village. He staged annual

53 *Heref. Times*, 6 Aug. 1836.
54 *Rep. Chief Registrar of Friendly Societies, 1875* (Parl. Papers, 1876 (424), lxix), pp. 270, 471.
55 *Rep. Chief Registrar of Friendly Societies, 1877* (Parl. Papers, 1878 (388), lxix), II, p. 12.
56 Ibid. p. 252.
57 *Rep. Chief Registrar of Friendly Societies, 1879* (Parl. Papers, 1889 (113), lxxxiv), II, p. 251.
58 *Rep. Chief Registrar of Friendly Societies, 1887* (Parl. Papers, 1878 (388), lxix), II, p. 130.
59 *Rep. Chief Registrar of Friendly Societies, 1911* (Parl. Papers, 1912–3 (123), lxxxi–lxxxii), Appendix N, II, p. 72.
60 Ibid.p. 73.

harvest suppers at the Winnings for between 100 and 300 guests, including employees, local landowners, and railway workers.[61] Ballard was also a keen supporter of the temperance movement, and built the Workmen's Hall in the early 1880s to provide an alcohol-free meeting place for working men,[62] and the adjoining Temperance Hotel was opened in 1882.[63] Fortnightly entertainment at the hall each winter included concerts, lectures, political meetings, and meetings of the Odd Fellows.[64] A Band of Hope was established there, and in 1882 it hosted a meeting which led to the creation of the Malvern Hills conservators.

A new public library and reading rooms were erected by the parish council in 1898, built on land adjacent to the Workmen's Hall owned by the Winnings Estate.[65] The Hill Institute, which was opened beneath the Church of the Good Shepherd in 1910, was used by soldiers recuperating at Brand Lodge during the First World War.[66] It closed in 1961, and later became a Working Men's Club, which closed in 1982.[67] Land in Mill Lane was conveyed by James Franck Bright of Brockbury to the rector for a parish hall in 1913,[68] and an army hut had been installed by 1922, replaced by a new building built by Allan Heywood Bright in 1927 as the Church Rooms (now known as the Village Hall) and St Crispin's chapel of ease.[69] It was refurbished and extended by the parish council c.1989.[70] The Workmen's Hall was converted into a popular club for the village youth after the Second World War.[71] A new library was built by the Walwyn Educational Foundation and leased to the local authority in 1957.[72] In 1991 the Foundation gave the library and the meadow in which it is located to the parish council, which administers it through the Walwyn Meadow Charity.[73] An extension to the library, the Millennium Room, opened in 2002.[74]

A horticultural society for Colwall and the neighbouring parishes had been founded by 1852, holding an exhibition in the village each year.[75] The Hill Institute established a Wyche and Upper Colwall show in 1942, which replaced the Colwall Village Show in the late 1950s.[76] The Wyche and Colwall Horticultural Society continues to organise an annual show.[77] A brass band was established at Perrycroft Lodge in 1900, with 15

61   Ballard, *Colwall Collection*, 44–6.
62   Above, Colwall Parish.
63   *Kelly's Dir.* (1885, 1895, 1909, 1917, 1922, 1926 edns).
64   R. Haig, *A History of Theatres & Performers in Herefs.* (Little Logaston, 2002), 93–4; *Worcs. Chron.* 13 Jan. 1883; 3 Feb. 1883; 13 June 1885; 18 Jan. 1896.
65   Ballard, *Colwall Collection*, 18–20.
66   CVS, F95, Hill Institute minute book, 1910–25.
67   CVS, F95, Hill institute minute books; B/19, George Grundy's letters; Inf from Mrs S. Bond
68   HAS, AE30/135.
69   Brooks and Pevsner, *Herefs.* 178.
70   HAS, CG36/4–5; CG36/8.
71   Ballard, *Colwall Collection*, 14–18.
72   Brooks and Pevsner, *Herefs.* 178; WAAS, 705.876 BA 8077, 26.
73   Charity Commission, no. 520945.
74   HAS, CG36/8 4 Sept. 2002.
75   *Worc. Jnl*, 19 Aug. 1852. In 1872 it was said that the society had been founded in 1847: ibid. 17 Aug. 1872.
76   D. Hodgson and P. Picton, unpubl. paper on the Wyche and Colwall Horticultural Society.
77   https://wychecolwallhorticulturalsoc.wordpress.com (accessed 13 Mar. 2018).

members,[78] which continued to function until 1953.[79] Perrycroft was purchased by the Birmingham Battalion of the Boys' Brigade in 1968,[80] as a residential activity centre, for which it was used up until 1998.[81] The Colwall Women's Institute, founded in 1930 with approximately 90 members, was closed in 2016,[82] when another WI group, Colwall Wings, was formed.[83] The Colwall Ladies Club was established with 57 members in 1986 to rival the all-male Probus Club, and continued to meet in 2019.[84] Colwall Village Society was established in 1998, to protect and improve the village environment, and to research and record village history.[85] It publishes a newsletter and pamphlets, holds meetings, and keeps an archive.

Inns and Alehouses

In 1619 three alehouse keepers were presented to the manorial court.[86] The equipment of William Lynton, 'Inn Holder', who died in 1689, included 'One hogs head, two half hogsheads, one firkin, one roundel, a dozen bottles, three earthen pots, one powdering tub and a skeel'.[87]

By the mid 19th century there were three public houses and two beer retailers in Colwall.[88] The Horse & Jockey was referred to in 1784, when it belonged to Thomas Gilding.[89] Known as the Horse & Groom by 1816, vestry meetings were intermittently held at the inn during the early 19th century.[90] It was an important public venue for auctions, cattle sales, pigeon racing matches, and lodge meetings.[91] In 1861 the contractor for the Malvern and Ledbury tunnels entertained 80 of his workmen at a dinner at the Horse & Groom.[92] Edward Allen and John Bray were both licensed as alehouse keepers in 1816, and still in 1828.[93] The latter presumably held the cottage at Chance's Pitch, shown on a map of *c*.1832,[94] which in 1841 was occupied by Thomas Bray innkeeper, and was later named the Wellington inn. In 1904 it was described as a brick-built house, with a separate bar and tap room, and a good garden.[95] Although the building is much older,

78   *Rep. Chief Registrar of Friendly Societies, 1911*, Appendix N, II, 74.
79   TNA, FS 15/1462; *London Gaz.* 24 July 1953.
80   *Colwall Clock*, Nov. 1980.
81   R. Bolton and P. Arkinstall, *Forward! The Birmingham Battalion of the Boys Brigade 1902–2002* (Aldridge, 2002), 102.
82   Inf. from Mrs S. Bond.
83   *Colwall Wings*, http://www.colwallwings.co.uk (accessed 21 Mar. 2018).
84   J Ingledew, 'Colwall Ladies Club', CVS (Colwall, 2001); http://www.colwallladiesclub.co.uk (accessed 8 Apr. 2019).
85   Inf. from John Atkin, Colwall Village Society.
86   HAS, AM33/8.
87   HAS, 106/3/5, will of William Lynton, 1689.
88   *Slater's Dir.* (1850 edn).
89   *Heref. Jnl*, 12 Feb. 1784; J. Eisel and R. Shoesmith, *The Pubs of Bromyard, Ledbury and East Herefs.* (Little Logaston, 2003), 266.
90   HAS, CK23/44.
91   *Heref. Jnl*, 10 Aug. 1867; *Worcs. Chron.* 7 July 1877.
92   *Worcs. Chron.* 25 Sept. 1861.
93   HAS, Q/CE/1.
94   GA, Q/Rum/129.
95   HAS, J33/42.

the Yew Tree is first noticed by that name in 1861.[96] Its landlord, Charles Pedlingham, changed the name to the Terrace inn for a period during the late 19th century.[97] It was later run by several generations of the Orgee family. In Upper Colwall, the Chase inn was first recorded in 1841,[98] and the Victoria Arms, a beerhouse near the summit of the Wyche, was recorded in 1861.[99] The Herefordshire House was in Upper Colwall in 1851 and 1861, but it had relocated to Malvern by 1911, taking the name the Wyche inn.[100] At the foot of the Herefordshire Beacon stood an inn known as the Wynd's Point by 1846,[101] and the British Camp by 1853.[102]

By the late 1870s there were four public houses competing for trade with a number of beerhouses.[103] One of these was the Crown inn on Walwyn Road in Colwall Stone, and another was the Royal Oak, also in Colwall Stone.[104] The Dog & Pheasant inn at Colwall Stone was demolished in 1879,[105] and the Railway inn, near the station, was another short-lived beerhouse in Colwall Stone.[106] Thomas Collis was described as a beer retailer in the census of 1881 and 1891, and may have been running a beerhouse from his home at Aston Cottage.[107] In 1905 there were three public houses – the British Camp, the Horse & Groom, and the Royal Oak – and four beerhouses, the Wellington, the Chase inn, the Crown, and the Yew Tree. The Royal Wells Brewery was a licensed wine and spirit merchant.[108] By 1941 the Horse & Groom reverted to its former name of the Horse & Jockey, which it remained, apart from a brief period when it was called the Oddfellows' Arms, until it was converted into a Thai restaurant in 2003.[109] In 2019 the Chase inn, the Crown, the Wellington, and the Yew Tree all remain open, and the Colwall Park Hotel and Malvern Hills Hotel also have public bars.

Sport

The Mathon and Colwall Hounds were established by William Bateson Cliffe before 1827.[110] Although based at the Shipping House, Mathon, the hunt's territory included the parish of Colwall. The hounds were relocated to Ledbury in 1834.[111] Colwall remained within the extensive territory hunted by the hounds,[112] who in the early 20th century met at Colwall Park Hotel and the British Camp inn.[113]

96   Census, 1861.
97   *Littlebury's Dir.* (1867 edn); Census, 1871.
98   Census, 1841.
99   Census, 1861.
100 Census, 1851; 1861; 1911
101 *Heref. Times*, 10 Oct. 1846.
102 *Heref. Times*, 20 Aug. 1853; *PO Dir.* (1856 edn).
103 *PO Dir.* (1879 edn); *Kelly's Dir.* (1895 edn).
104 HAS, D96/12; D100.
105 Ballard, *Colwall Collection*, 13.
106 *Littlebury's Dir.* (1867 edn); *Worcs. Chron.* 20 Apr. 1870.
107 Eisel and Shoesmith, *Pubs of Bromyard, Ledbury and East Herefs.* 266
108 HAS, G56/8.
109 Eisel and Shoesmith, *Pubs of Bromyard, Ledbury and East Herefs.* 266; inf. from current tenants
110 *Berks. Chron.* 3 Feb. 1827; *Worc. Jnl,* 3 Mar. 1894.
111 Pinches, *Ledbury: a Market Town,* 140–1.
112 *Glouc. Citizen,* 28 Feb. 1928.
113 CVS, H17.

Figure 22 *Aerial photograph of Colwall Park Racecourse, Colwall Stone, 1933.*

Horseracing was established in Colwall in 1877, in a field near to the Horse & Groom, when foot races were also run.[114] The horse races were still being held in the 1890s.[115] Roland Cave-Browne-Cave established a racecourse at Colwall in 1900, in concert with a number of other ventures, as part of an effort to reinvigorate his estate.[116] A three-mile course was laid out south of the railway station, and a grandstand was erected.[117] The first meet, held in May 1900, attracted 3,000 people, some of whom were carried by special services laid on by the Great Western Railway.[118] Meets were subsequently held three times a year, in May, October and December. Colwall Park Race Course Ltd was liquidated in 1943.[119] Attempts to resume racing after the war met with limited success,[120] and the North Ledbury Hunt used the racecourse for point-to-point meetings

114 *Heref. Times,* 8 Sept. 1877.
115 *Worc. Jnl,* 13 July 1895.
116 N. Neve, *National Hunt Racing at Colwall Park Racecourse 1900–39* (Colwall, 1995).
117 *Worc. Jnl,* 12 May 1900.
118 *Worc. Jnl,* 5 May 1900.
119 *London Gaz.* 26 Feb. 1943.
120 TNA, BT 31/38131/454439.

Figure 23 *Photograph of Colwall Rangers Football Club in1929.*

in the early 1960s.[121] After the last races were held in April 1963, the site was returned to agriculture.[122]

Cave-Browne-Cave also established a golf course near his racecourse, with a club house at Stone Farm. It opened in 1908,[123] but closed three years later on the bankruptcy of Cave-Brown-Cave. The South Herefordshire Club was founded in the same year at a site near Evendine Lane and incorporated some of the former links,[124] but closed at the end of 1915.[125]

A cricket match took place on Colwall Green in 1849 between schoolboys of Ledbury and Colwall.[126] Further matches were reported between a Colwall XI, who played at the Lower Hardwick Pleck near Grubend, against Hereford College in 1857,[127] Bishop's Froome in 1859,[128] and Malvern Wells and Eastnor in 1862.[129] One individual expressed his concerns in 1863 that the recent enclosure of small plots from Colwall Green endangered the future of what had for many years been 'the poor boys' playground' for cricket.[130] A second team, called the Colwall Knickerbockers and representing the grammar school, had been formed by 1867, when it played matches against Malvern

---

121 *Farm & Country*, 14 Feb. 1962, 13.
122 *Birmingham Post*, 16 Apr. 1966.
123 *Glos. Echo*, 25 Apr. 1908.
124 *Heref. Times*, 17 June 1911.
125 TNA, BT 31/13668/117011; *Western Mail*, 18 Dec. 1915.
126 *Heref. Jnl*, 13 June 1849.
127 *Heref. Times*, 26 Sept. 1857.
128 *Malvern Advertiser*, 30 July 1859; *Heref. Times*, 13 Aug. 1859.
129 *Heref. Times*, 2 Aug. 1862; 27 Sept. 1862.
130 *Heref. Jnl*, 13 June 1863.

College and Colwall cricket club.[131] By 1876 the school's team were called the Colwall Lilies.[132] Colwall played in the Three Counties Cricket League until 1998, when they joined the newly formed Worcestershire County Cricket League. Their home matches are played at Stowe Lane.[133]

The village is important nationally in the development of women's cricket. In 1926 members of the All-England Women's Hockey Association spent a week at Colwall, during which they played friendly cricket matches in Cheltenham and Malvern. This led directly to the establishment of the Women's Cricket Association, which organised women's cricket until 1998. An annual week-long festival of women's cricket has been organised in Colwall since 1927.[134]

Colwall Rangers Football Club had been formed by 1887, when matches were arranged against teams from Worcestershire.[135] In the following year, a charity concert was arranged at the Workmen's Hall to raise funds for the club.[136] By 1894 the club was a member of the Worcester and District Charity Football Association, and by the 1930s it had joined the Malvern District League. A proposal was made in 1967 to provide a new football ground for the village on the west side of the green.[137] In 1998 football was transferred from Walwyn Meadow to Colwall Green.[138] By the 21st century the club had joined the Herefordshire League,[139] but appears to have folded in 2009.[140] In 2019, two Sunday League teams, Colwall Wanderers and Colwall St James, competed in the Worcester & District Football League.[141]

Education

There has been an endowed grammar school at Colwall since the 17th century, subsequently becoming the Elms School. In the early 19th century day-schools were established, and later two church schools, Colwall Hill school, originally for boys, and Colwall Valley school, originally for girls and infants. In the second half of the 20th century the schools were reorganised. The parish has other notable private schools.

Walwyn's Free Grammar School, now The Elms School

Humphry Walwyn left £600 to the Grocers' Company in 1614 to purchase property in London, the rent from which was to be used to establish a free school in Colwall.[142] The management of the school was to be vested in the Grocers' Company, who were to

131 *Heref. Jnl*, 29 June 1867.
132 *Worc. Jnl*, 10 June 1876.
133 http://www.colwallcc.co.uk/about-ccc (accessed 9 Apr. 2019).
134 R. Heyhoe Flint and N. Rheinberg, *Fair Play* (1976), 30–3.
135 *Worcs. Chron.* 24 Dec. 1887; 31 Dec. 1887.
136 *Worcs. Chron.* 1 Dec. 1888.
137 HAS, CG36/1, 11 Jan. 1967.
138 HAS, CG36/7, 21 Sept. 1998.
139 *Heref. Times*, 3 May 2000.
140 The last mention of the club in the parish magazine dates from June 2009: *Colwall Clock*, June 2009.
141 Worcester & District Football League, http://worcesterleague.com (accessed 30 Sep. 2019).
142 TNA, PROB 11/123/103; *Rep. City of London Livery Companies Commission, IV* (1884), 100; *The Endowed Charities of the City of London* (1829), 236–7. P. Hurle, *Portrait of a School: The Elms in Colwall 1614–2000* (Colwall, 2000).

choose the master, and visit the school every three years to examine the scholars. The master was to teach the poor children of Colwall and seven from Little Malvern for free, and was not to charge wealthier parents more than 10s. a year. The master was to be godly, to make prayers twice a day, to catechise his pupils, and to preach once a quarter at Colwall and once a year at Little Malvern. In return, he was to have the whole profits of the endowment, excluding annual legacies of £5 each left to the Grocers' Company and to the parish of Chipping Ongar (Essex).

No property was purchased with Walwyn's legacy; instead, £30 a year was charged upon eight houses already owned by the Company, to be paid to the master. A large farmhouse and 3 a. of land, purchased before 1622, was used as the school house.[143] Besides the master's salary, the Grocers committed to the costs of repairing and maintaining the schoolhouse, making frequent payments, including a grant of 20 marks (£13 3s.4d.) in 1647 to repair damage caused during the Civil War.[144] The first schoolmaster was Richard Walwyn, the nephew of the founder, appointed in 1623.[145] He was still there in 1640, when he witnessed a will,[146] but died before the Restoration. He was succeeded by his son Henry,[147] who died in 1670, and then the rector John Haylings who died soon afterwards. Haylings' successor at both the rectory and in the schoolhouse was John Page, a clergyman who also held benefices at Coddington and Eastnor.[148] The teaching of Robert Symonds, appointed master in 1759,[149] was so unsatisfactory that the parishioners unsuccessfully petitioned the Grocers for his replacement.[150]

The schoolhouse was rebuilt in 1796, and a room for boarders was added in 1808. The master in 1818, George Wallett, converted the school into a private boarding school, and very few of the parishioners were admitted.[151] He was only dismissed when the Company agreed to give him a pension of £50 a year.[152] There were 52 free pupils at the school c.1821, and the syllabus consisted of English, arithmetic, and religious instruction, with no classical element.[153] The master's salary was augmented by a grant of £5 6s. 8d. by the Crown from the land revenue in Herefordshire.[154] Under the mastership of Thomas Dean, the school's reputation improved,[155] and there were 68 pupils c.1835.[156]

A new elementary schoolroom was built for the free pupils in 1851, dividing them from the fee-paying pupils.[157] The elementary school was deemed in 1867 to be appropriate for the children of farmers and labourers that attended, offering a better

---

143 Hurle, *The Elms*, 12, 17–9.
144 Hurle, *The Elms*, 13-4;
145 Hurle, *The Elms*, 13; *CCED*, no. 174331.
146 HAS, 050/3/20 will of Anne Turner, 1637.
147 *CCED*, no. 174332.
148 *CCED*, no. 173040.
149 *CCED*, no. 166360.
150 Hurle, *The Elms*, 23–6
151 *Educ. of Poor Digest, 1818* (Parl. Papers, 1819 (224), ix), p. 331.
152 *Endowed Charities of London*, 236.
153 *Endowed Charities of London*, 236.
154 *Endowed Charities of London*, 237.
155 *32nd Rep. Coms. of Inquiry into Charities* (Parl. Papers, 1837–8 (140), xxvi), p. 103.
156 *Education Enquiry Abstract, 1835* (Parl. Papers, 1835 (62), xli), p. 339.
157 Hurle, *The Elms*, 28–9, 32; Guildhall Library, CLC/L/GH/G/056A.

standard than a National School.[158] The master, Robert Carter, who lived in the house adjacent to the school, was regarded as the visitor of the school and was allowed to teach private boarders. The teaching at the elementary school was undertaken by a second master and an usher, paid £100 and £30 a year respectively by the Grocers'. There were 63 boys registered at the elementary school in 1867, of whom only four were aged 14 or above. Besides the traditional subjects, the syllabus comprised history and geography, with drawing, mensuration and surveying for the oldest boys. To support his private school, Robert Carter built a new schoolhouse and dormitories. Carter's successor, Charles Black (headmaster 1876–1910) was the first chairman of the Incorporated Association of Preparatory Schools.[159] By this date the elementary school could accommodate 87 pupils, although the average attendance was 54.[160] In the year 1875–6 the school received a government grant worth c.£42 and contributions from the Grocers of £195. By 1893 the school could accommodate 121, although average attendance was only 62.[161]

In 1904 the managers of the grammar school were accused of incompetence. Like his predecessor, Black was running a large preparatory school called the Elms at his home, to the detriment of the free school.[162] In 1909 a new scheme for the management of the school was adopted,[163] which formally divided the elementary school from the private preparatory school.[164] A new body of 12 governors was constituted under the name of the Walwyn's Free School and Exhibition Foundation, comprising three representatives of the Grocers, two of the county council, three of the parish, one of the Little Malvern parish meeting, one to be appointed by the rector and churchwardens of Colwall, and two co-optative governors. The Grocers agreed to contribute £2,000 to the foundation in repayment of Walwyn's original bequest. Loud objections were raised in the parish at such a small sum, and the matter was raised in the House of Lords, but the Board of Education determined that it was the most that could be achieved.[165] Of this sum, £600 was to be dedicated to the improvement and maintenance of the elementary school, and the remainder supported exhibitions of up to £10 for children of Colwall or Little Malvern to attend secondary or agricultural school, and up to £50 for higher education. Following the closure of the boys' school, a new scheme of 1954 established the Walwyn Educational Foundation, to support needy boys and girls of Colwall or Little Malvern to attend a secondary school, technical college, university, or another institution of further education.[166] Following an amendment in 2007, the foundation provides small grants to young persons from Colwall or Little Malvern who are undertaking tertiary education.[167]

158 *15th Rep. Royal Com. to inquire into Education in Schools in England and Wales* (Parl. Papers, 1867–8 [3966], xiv), 211.
159 Hurle, *The Elms*, 44
160 *Return of Public Elementary Schools, 1877* (Parl. Papers, 1887 [Cd 1882], lxvii), 94–5.
161 *Return of Public Elementary Schools, 1892–3* (Parl. Papers, 1894 [C 7529], lxv), 226–7.
162 *Kelly's Dir.* (1876–7, 1885, 1891, 1900, 1905 edns).
163 *Scheme for the Management of Walwyn's Free School, 1909* (Parl. Papers, 1909 (22), lxvii).
164 Below, The Elms.
165 Hurle, *The Elms, 56. Hansard*, HL Deb. 1 Apr. 1909, I, cc. 584–92.
166 WAAS, 468 BA11858/4.
167 Charity Commission, no. 527152.

Elementary Education

The Free School was the only school in the parish until 1828, when a day school was established, supported by subscriptions, and also a Sunday school, supported entirely by the curate, Thomas Dean.[168] In 1835 the day school was attended by eight boys and 31 girls and the Sunday school by 60 children of both sexes. The day school was presumably that later referred to as the girl's schoolroom, where vestry meetings were held in the 1840s,[169] but it may have ceased to be used when the new elementary schoolroom was opened at the free school. A new girls' schoolroom, later known as the Hill school, was erected by the rector in Upper Colwall in 1856,[170] and another, later known as the Valley school, was opened on Colwall Green in 1866.[171] In 1877 the Valley school, which could accommodate 117 children, had an average attendance of 50,[172] which had risen to 61 by 1893, when the Hill school had an average attendance of 70.[173] The Valley school was extended in 1894, to comprise two rooms, one for the infants and one for the juniors.[174]

In 1902 the Valley school had 69 girls and 54 infants on its registers, with an average attendance of 62 and 38 respectively, who were taught by three certified teachers and two monitors.[175] The school received *c.*£179 a year in grants and *c.*£70 from subscriptions.[176] In the same year there were 38 girls and 45 infants registered at the Hill school, with an average attendance of 33 and 37 respectively, taught by two teachers and two monitors.[177] By 1906 there was also an evening school attended by 24 adults, supported with an annual grant of £5 4*s.* 6*d.*[178] In 1914 there were 57 girls over the age of seven at Valley school, and 41 infants of both sexes, while two years later there were 60 children, including seven under the age of five, enrolled at the Hill school.[179] Two years later the curriculum included cookery and domestic science, laundry and housewifery, dairy work, handicraft, light woodwork, and gardening.[180] Due to food shortages during the First World War, dinners were provided at Colwall's schools in 1918.[181] It was usual in Colwall to arrange the school holidays to coincide with the hop-picking season, and some children were also expected to be available earlier in the summer to pick fruit.[182]

In 1929 the Valley school employed three teachers and a monitor, while one teacher was employed at the Hill school.[183] The county council began reorganising Herefordshire's schools from 1929, although there was some resistance to this in Colwall over the question of continuing Church of England instruction after the

---

168 *Education Enquiry Abstract, 1835*, 339.
169 HAS, CK23/44.
170 CERC, NS/7/1/3384.
171 CERC, NS/7/1/3383.
172 *Return of Public Elementary Schools, 1877*, 95–6.
173 *Return of Public Elementary Schools, 1893* (Parl. Papers, 1894 [C 7529], lxv), pp. 226–7.
174 HAS, AK78/62–66.
175 HAS, AK78/36.
176 HAS, AK78/62–66.
177 HAS, AK78/36.
178 *List of Evening Schools in England and Wales, 1906* (Parl. Papers, 1907 [Cd 3314], lxii), p. 31.
179 HAS, AK78/34.
180 HAS, AK78/49.
181 HAS, AK78/34.
182 HAS, AK78/34, 69.
183 HAS, AK78/38.

reorganisation.[184] In 1933 the boys' school was attended by 49 boys, the Valley school by 92 infants and older girls, and the Hill school by another 18 girls, and a proposal was made to close the latter.[185] By this date, though, the Valley school was felt to be obsolete, and a petition was drawn calling for the county's LEA to take control of the school, and provide it with modern accommodation.[186] Despite this the school remained the responsibility of the parish, which could not take on such ambitious work, instead improving the ventilation, installing new heating, and replacing rotten floor boards.[187]

Instead of closing, the Hill school became an infants' school, and in 1951 there were 24 children at the Hill school aged between five and eight years.[188] The Valley school continued to have an infants' department, and also took older children from the parish.[189] After the Second World War a hut was erected behind the main building to accommodate a mixed class of pupils aged 14 and over. In 1948 there were 33 pupils at the boys' school aged between nine and 14, whose curriculum included woodwork, art and music, and who kept beehives on the grounds.[190] The boys transferred to the Valley school at the age of 14, until 1953 when the two schools were amalgamated, although the two sites continued to be used for a time.[191] The school also accommodated children from Coddington parish at the age of 11, and all children over 13 were transferred to the secondary school at Canon Frome.

In the 1970s the Hill and Valley schools were amalgamated to create Colwall CE Primary School. Colwall was shortlisted for the provision of a new school building in 1972,[192] but instead the Valley school was rebuilt c.1981,[193] and the Hill school closed in 1982.[194] Early in 1992 there were 140 pupils on the primary school roll, near capacity,[195] and by 1997 there were 156 children at the school,[196] where accommodation was becoming so cramped that two additional temporary classrooms were necessary.[197] In 2014 the school had to move into temporary accommodation because of an extreme damp problem,[198] and in 2018 it moved into new premises next to the village hall on Mill Lane.[199] The school has capacity for 210 pupils with 158 on the roll.[200]

The Elms

After the establishment of Walwyn's Free School upon its new foundation in 1909, the Elms continued as an entirely separate private preparatory school. The buildings

184 HAS, AK78/29.
185 HAS, AK78/33.
186 HAS, AK78/69.
187 HAS, AK78/68–9.
188 HAS, AK78/33; CJ45/3/41.
189 HAS, CJ45/3/40.
190 HAS, CJ45/3/39.
191 HAS, CJ45/3/42.
192 HAS, CG36/1.
193 HAS, CG36/2.
194 HAS, CG36/9; *Hansard*, HC Deb. 16 Feb. 1982, XVIII, cc. 109–12W.
195 HAS, CG36/5.
196 HAS, CG36/6, 10 Dec. 1997.
197 HAS, CG36/5; CG36/7.
198 *Heref. Times*, 6 Oct. 2014.
199 *Malvern Gaz.* 10 Jan. 2018.
200 Inf. provided by Colwall Church of England Primary School.

remained the property of the free school foundation, and the rent paid by the headmaster for the facilities provided the income for the foundation. In 1911, besides the classrooms and the dormitories, which could accommodate 35, the school had a chapel, carpenter's shop, gymnasium, fives court, an open-air swimming pool, and a separate sanatorium.[201] The syllabus consisted of English, mathematics, Latin, Greek, French, German, and drawing. In 1943 the school was purchased by William Singleton, headmaster since 1916, who was responsible for its post-war development.[202] He left the school to his sons, who in 1965 gave up ownership to a new charitable trust.[203] About 1985 it merged with Seaford Court school of Malvern Link, and was initially known as the Elms with Seaford Court but reverted to its original name.[204] It maintains a close connection with the Grocers' Company, receiving financial assistance from them. In 2019 it was a co-educational, independent preparatory school for children aged three to 13.

Evendine Court School of Domestic Economy

The artist and traveller Marian Buck founded a school to teach girls domestic economy at Camp End on Jubilee Drive in 1896.[205] The school's popularity necessitated a move to a larger building at Evendine Court, modelled on a large country house.[206] The curriculum included domestic economy, horticulture, dairying and poultry-keeping. In 1909, when the school was bought by Miss Baird of West Malvern, the school's curriculum included cookery, housework, elementary hygiene, laundry, millinery, dressmaking, and the care of household linen.[207] By 1957 the out-dated curriculum was said to be deterring girls from attending, and the premises were also in need of modernisation.[208] Evendine Court, later classified as a finishing school, closed in 1999.

The Downs School

The Downs School was founded by the Quakers Herbert and Ethel Jones in 1900 as a preparatory boarding school for boys.[209] Several members of staff and a number of early pupils were also Quakers, including children of the Cadbury and Rowntree families. The school was extended in the 1920s with the addition of a quadrangle.[210] Geoffrey Hoyland, headmaster from 1920, developed an innovative curriculum, and established the Downs Light Railway, a miniature railway located in the school grounds, to educate the pupils which survives in 2019, supported by a charitable trust.[211] The poet W. H. Auden taught at the school between 1932 and 1935, where he wrote, composed, founded a school magazine called *The Badger*, and organised a musical revue in which the whole school

201 *War Office Times and Naval Review*, 1 May 1911, 18–9.
202 HAS, AK40/31/1; Hurle, *The Elms*, 57–9.
203 Hurle, *The Elms*, 94.
204 Hurle, *The Elms*, 109–11.
205 TNA, ED 197/3; *VCH Herefs. Bosbury*, 14, 55.
206 Brooks and Pevsner, *Herefs.* 181.
207 J. Butchart, *Ninety Years On: a History of Evendine Court* (Malvern, 1986).
208 TNA, ED 197/3.
209 P. Bevan, 'A Quaker Tradition – a brief history of Quakers in the Malvern area', *Malvern Quakers Newsletter* (Summer 2013), 5–7; E.J. Brown, *The First Five: The Story of a School* (Printed privately, 1987).
210 Brooks and Pevsner, *Herefs.* 179.
211 http://www.dlrtrust.btck.co.uk (accessed 23 Oct. 2019); Charity Commission no. 513882.

Figure 24 *'Tubby', the Downs Light Railway's first steam locomotive, at 'Windermere' in 1949.*

performed.[212] In 2008 the school merged with Hillstone preparatory school in Malvern to form the Downs Malvern preparatory school.

Other Schools

In 1914 a day prep school for girls at Malvernhurst moved to West Malvern Road and became the Wychcrest Private Junior School for Girls.[213] It closed in 1958 upon the retirement of the headmistress, after which it was a school for children in care until 1985, when it ceased to be a school.

Social Welfare

Charities for the Poor

Poor's Lands

The survey of 1577 recorded five pieces of 'parish land' abutting the lands of the bishop's tenants, perhaps the origin of the later poor's land.[214] A second-hand copy of an early 17th-century feoffment of the lands, extant in 1810, listed *c.*22 a. of land, a messuage, and

212 *ODNB*, s.v. W.H. Auden, poet (accessed 30 Sept. 2019).
213 Marsh, *The Commercial Complex On West Malvern Road*, 12.
214 HAS, AA59/A/2, ff. 64, 69, 73, 74v, 79v.

the church house which in 1614 belonged to the poor.[215] Because the names of the donors and the uses to which they had originally donated had been forgotten, and because it was impossible to identify any heirs of former feoffees, it proved impossible to register the lands. By *c*.1837 only 18 a. could certainly be identified, and the annual rents, the profits of which had been distributed to the poor, had fallen from £5–6 a year to £3 18*s*. The Charity Commissioners estimated that the land would be worth £20 a year if let at commercial rates, but that the loss of all documentation by the parish had enabled the tenants to continue paying the inadequate ancient rents.

Other Charities

Robert Bright (d. 1665) of Brockbury bequeathed 15*s*. a year to be paid to the poor from his estate.[216] Henry Bright (d. 1777) of Ham Green (Som.) bequeathed £100 to the parish, charged upon Court farm in Coddington, the annual interest of which produced £4 a year, distributed to the poor in doles worth 2*s*. 6*d*. on St Thomas' Day (21 December).[217] The funds were distributed up to 1838, but there is no further record of the charity.[218] Elizabeth Brydges of Ledbury left £150 to Colwall,[219] the interest from which produced £4 10*s*. a year in 1837, which was distributed to the poor in doles of bread each quarter.[220] Lowbridge Bright left the annual interest of £500, worth £19 11*s*. 6*d*. in 1837, to distribute coal to the poor not receiving parish relief, of the parishes of Colwall and Coddington.'[221] The income fell to £17 17*s*. 8*d*. by 1895.[222] This charity was supplemented by that of Elizabeth Rosetta Peyton, who bequeathed £166 13*s*. 1*d*. to provide coal to the ten poorest and most infirm cottagers in the parish.[223] A clothing club operated between 1899 and 1956. Members paid ½*d*. a year to join, and 4*d*. a month to the rector. Only one member of a family could join.[224]

Several charities had been lost to Colwall by 1837. Blanch Hartland left £4 in 1664 to remain as stock for the poor; the last payment was made in 1802.[225] Mary Pewtrice devised a cottage and garden in Evendine Street to Richard Hill and his heirs in her will of 1724, subject to the annual payment of 4*s*. to the parish for the use of the poor. The rentcharge had been lost by 1810 'by the negligence of the parish officers.' In 1704, William Brydges left £86 to purchase land, the profits from which were to be used to buy bread for poor churchgoers of Colwall and Coddington.[226] The charity fell into abeyance with the sale of the property to James Martin.[227] In 1861 Thomas Brassey and Stephen

215 *32nd Rep. Coms. of Inquiry into Charities*, 103–8; H. Meates, *Rep. Colwall Charities* (Worc. 1895); HAS, T9/39.
216 HAS, AE30/354.
217 TNA, PROB 11/1053/390; HAS, AE30/1; *32nd Rep. Coms. of Inquiry into Charities*, 108.
218 Meates, *Colwall Charities*, 12.
219 TNA, PROB 11/1462/217.
220 TNA, PROB 11/1053/390; HAS, AE30/1; *32nd Rep. Coms. of Inquiry into Charities*, 108.
221 *32nd Rep. Coms. of Inquiry into Charities*, 109.
222 Meates, *Colwall Charities*, 15.
223 Ibid.
224 HAS, CK23/62.
225 *32nd Rep. Coms. of Inquiry into Charities*, 109; Meates, *Colwall Charities*, 16.
226 TNA, PROB 11/479/480.
227 *Worc. Jnl*, 31 Aug. 1820; *Morning Advertiser*, 7 Oct. 1820; *32nd Rep. Coms. of Inquiry into Charities*, 109.

Ballard, the engineers constructing the Hereford-Worcester railway, gave 50 tons of coal to the poor of Colwall to celebrate the completion of the line.[228]

Poor Relief

Poor Relief Before 1834

During the 18th century relief of the poor mainly consisted of regular doles of money, although payments were made for specific purposes, and clothes and fuel were also distributed. In 1732–3 three individuals were each given 5s. during a period of sickness, a child was given a pair of shoes, and a woman was paid to prepare a widow's body for burial. Twelve paupers, including several children, were receiving weekly payments of out-relief in 1759.[229] Cottages owned by the parish, including the former church house, were used to house the poor, who paid reduced or no rent.[230] In 1800 a committee of the vestry established to consider the high price of corn and flour decided that both would be purchased with money from the poor rate and sold to the poor at a reduced cost.[231] Between November 1800 and August 1801 the sale of wheat, barley, rye flour, meal, peas, beans, and potatoes to the poor resulted in a loss to the parish of £155 13s. 3½d.[232] The policy of selling food at a reduced rate to the poor of the parish continued until the adoption of the new poor law in 1834.[233] In 1801 50 individuals, including children, received sums of between 1s. and 5s. per week, the majority receiving 2s. a week.[234] In January 1821 a child was sent to the deaf and dumb asylum in London, the cost of his travel and clothing being met from the poor rates and by subscription.[235]

Medical Services

Until the 19th century medical services had to be sought at Ledbury or Malvern. The Ledbury poor-law union appointed medical officers for the district, whose duties included vaccination of the public.[236] A dispensary was established in Colwall by the Great Malvern surgeon Mervin Coates in 1847, for the benefit of the poor of Colwall and Coddington.[237] From the late 19th century medical practitioners began to establish themselves in the parish, beginning with the arrival c.1897 of the doctor Samuel McMillan Challinor, who soon joined the parish council.[238] A pharmacy had opened by 1909,[239] and in 1911 there were three doctors resident in the parish.[240] In 2019 there was a doctor's surgery on the site of the former vinegar works near Stone Drive.

228 *Heref. Times,* 10 Aug. 1861, 8; *Heref. Jnl,* 14 Aug. 1861, 3; Ballard, *Colwall Collections,* 40.
229 HAS, AE30/425.
230 Below, Local Government.
231 HAS, CK23/44, pp. 18–9.
232 HAS, CK23/44, p. 20.
233 HAS, CK23/44.
234 HAS, CK23/44, p. 10.
235 HAS, CK23/44, p. 233.
236 *Worc. Jnl,* 10 Sept. 1846.
237 HAS, K42/348, p. 123.
238 *The Medical Register* (1899), 328; HAS, T9/58, 9 May 1900.
239 *Kelly's Dir.* (1909 edn).
240 *The Medical Register* (1911 edn), 214, 474, 696.

RELIGIOUS HISTORY

THE PARISH PROBABLY HAD ITS origins as part of the extensive *parochia* of the Anglo-Saxon minster at Ledbury.[1] The patron is the bishop of Hereford and rectors were often absentee members of the cathedral chapter. From the 17th century curates have often also served as masters of the free school. There was little history of Nonconformity or Catholicism in the parish until the 1830s, when several Nonconformist meetings were licensed. The lack of a dominant resident Anglican landowner and the parish's rural location provided an ideal setting for the growth of Nonconformity. From the mid 19th century, several new places of worship were erected in the parish, in particular in Upper Colwall.

Church Origins and Parochial Organisation

Although the first documentary evidence of a church at Colwall dates from the 12th century, a small amount of reused Anglo-Saxon material suggests that a church probably stood on the site at least a century earlier.[2] Like Bosbury the parish was probably originally served from the mother church of Ledbury.[3] The proximity of the church to the bishop's manor house suggests that it originated as a manorial church. The dedication of the church to St James is only recorded in the early 19th century.[4]

There was no change in the ecclesiastical parish boundaries until the late 20th century.[5] The benefice was renamed Colwall with Upper Colwall in 1925, when a grant of £650 was made by the Ecclesiastical Commissioners (matched by an identical sum raised by the parishioners) to supplement the stipend of the curate serving Upper Colwall.[6] Under the terms of the grant, if Upper Colwall were ever to become a separate parish the income was to cover the new incumbent's stipend. Instead, in 1982 the benefice was united with Coddington to create Colwall with Upper Colwall and Coddington.[7] The bishop remains the patron, and the rectory in Colwall became the residence of the united benefice.[8]

1   S. Pinches, *Ledbury: People and Parish*, 32.
2   Below, church architecture.
3   S.K. Waddington, 'The Anglo-Saxon mother churches of eastern Herefs', *TWNFC*, 62 (2014), 76–7.
4   HAS, CF50/243.
5   LPL, ECE/11/1.
6   LPL, ECE/7/1/27443/1; *Lond. Gaz.* 30 Oct. 1925, p. 7051.
7   LPL, D646731.
8   Inf. from Sarah Girling, Pastoral Secretary, Heref. Dioc.

Advowson and Church Endowment

The patronage of the living, which remains a rectory, has been vested in the bishop of
Hereford since the earliest times. The king presented in 1389 and 1492, during vacancies
in the see.[9] The archbishop of Canterbury presented in 1789, having claimed his right to
the next presentation of a benefice in the gift of the bishop upon the latter's election in
the previous year.[10]

The value of the benefice was assessed at £10 in 1291,[11] and the ninth of corn,
wool and lambs was valued at 60s. c.1342.[12] The tithes and offerings of the parish were
valued at £20 6s. 8d. in 1535,[13] and the glebe comprised c.66 a. in the late 16th century.[14]
The parsonage was let by successive rectors on long leases from at least the mid 16th
century.[15] It was said to be worth about £100 c.1607, when it was let on a 90-year lease,
the lessee paying the rector an annual rent of £20 6s. 8d.[16] It was valued at £95 in 1656,[17]
and it was valued at c.£76 in 1663.[18] The living was said to be worth c.£130 in 1763,[19]
and £155 in 1831. The rector's tithes were commuted for a rent charge of £448 9s. a year
in 1840,[20] when the glebe was found to measure c.62 a.[21] The rector's income was said
to be £530 a year in 1868, of which £454 was the value of the tithes.[22] The income of the
living fell to £360 by 1908.[23] It was augmented in 1915 with an annual grant of £30 by the
Ecclesiastical Commissioners, on the condition that the rector employ an assistant curate
with a salary of £120 a year.[24] In 1932 the rector's income amounted to £564, of which the
glebe was worth £19, grants by the Ecclesiastical Commissioners £83, fees £10, and the
Easter offerings £20.[25]

Rectory House

The rectory comprised a messuage with a dovecote and fishponds c.1342.[26] It was
described as 'defective in the roof, walls, shutters and in other ways' in 1397;[27] complaints
of defects were raised again in 1423.[28] In the early 17th century the rectory comprised

9   *Cal. Pat. 1377–81*, 347; *Reg. Myllying*, 201.
10   LPL, VB 1/12, p. 81; *CCED*, nos 21260, 103935.
11   *Tax. Eccl.* (Rec. Com.), 160.
12   *Inq. Non.* (Rec. Com.), 153.
13   *Valor Eccl.* III, 48.
14   HAS, HD2/1/28.
15   TNA, C 2/JasI/B19/71.
16   Ibid.
17   LPL, COMM.XIIa/10, f. 3; *Herefs. Militia Assessments*, 94.
18   LPL, VB 1/10, p. 79; *CCED*, no. 34844.
19   LPL, VB 1/15, p. 210; *CCED*, no. 22038.
20   TNA, IR 29/14/52.
21   HAS, AA26/III/3.
22   *Crockford's Clerical Dir.* (1868), 165.
23   *Crockford's Clerical Dir.* (1908), 237.
24   *Lond. Gaz.* 9 July 1915, p. 6720; HAS, HD10/107.
25   *Crockford's Clerical Dir.* (1932), 268.
26   *Inq. Non.* (Rec. Com.), 153.
27   A.T. Bannister, 'Visitation returns of the diocese of Hereford in 1397: Part III', *Eng. Hist. Rev.*, LXV
     (1930), 92.
28   *Reg. Spofford*, 37.

the house, two barns, a byre for cattle, two gardens, and an orchard.[29] The parsonage house, called new in 1663,[30] was assessed for one hearth in 1665.[31]

The rectory became dilapidated during the incumbency of the insolvent Thomas Wynne (rector 1830–39).[32] It was rebuilt on the same site, near the church, c.1841.It was designed by Samuel Daukes (1811–80) in a Tudor Gothic style, with three gabled bays, the larger central bay projecting forwards,[33] and it was funded by a mortgage of £1,595 from Queen Anne's Bounty.[34] The house was enlarged in 1922–3, and again in 1931–3.[35] The house was sold c.1932,[36] and became a private residence called Glebe House. By c.1954 the rectory was a modern house on the Walwyn Road, Colwall.[37]

Religious Life

Middle Ages to Reformation

As a benefice in the gift of the bishop, the living was often held by functionaries and minor canons of the cathedral chapter, many of whom had little or no involvement with the daily life of the parish. There were frequent exchanges of the living with other clerical administrators, and it is likely that the incumbent was rarely resident. Instead curates, whose identities are generally unknown, would usually have served the religious needs of the parish.

The earliest references to clerics at Colwall come from the late 12th century (see the Appendix for a list of known rectors from 1171 to 1840). Adam, priest of Colwall, witnessed a grant of land to the priory of Little Malvern 1171 x 1178.[38] His probable successor, Walter of Colwall, was a clerk and probably also the steward of Bishop Robert Foliot 1179 x 1186.[39] The first priest to be described as rector was Gerard of Eugines, referred to in 1276, who was probably a confidant or relative of Bishop Peter of Aigueblanche.[40] The first curate who can be named was John Comyn, who was one of six parishioners presented for adultery in 1397, having cohabited with another man's wife for six years. Comyn was also accused of having falsified the testament of a parishioner who had died two years before, to acquire 9 marks in silver and other goods belonging to her. In that year it was also recorded that lamps were maintained within the church before the Crucifixion and the Blessed Virgin Mary.[41]

From the 16th century it is possible to glimpse more of the religious life of the parish. The will of John Viall, rector from 1515 until his death in 1525, demonstrates

29   HAS, HD2/1/28.
30   *Herefs. Militia Assessments*, 94.
31   HAS, AM29/1 TS, p. 70.
32   HER, 35399.
33   Brooks and Pevsner, *Herefs.* 176–7; *The Builder*, 20 Mar. 1880, 366; 22 May 1880, 650; NHLE, no. 1082149, Glebe House (accessed 30 Sept. 2019).
34   HAS, HD8/16–7.
35   LPL, QAB/7/6/E5493.
36   LPL, QAB/7/5/K10495.
37   HAS, T17/1; inf. from Susan Lawson, assistant to the Bp. of Heref.
38   Dugdale, *Mon.* IV, 449–50; *VCH Warks.* V, 190.
39   *Fasti Eccles. Ang.* 1066–1300, VIII, 92.
40   *Reg. Cantilupe*, xxvi, 86; *Fasti Eccles. Ang.* 1066–1300, VIII, 98.
41   Bannister, 'Visitation returns of Hereford, 1397', 92.

his slender connections with Colwall. As a member of the cathedral chapter, he usually resided in Hereford, where he owned property, and he made elaborate provisions for his funeral in the cathedral. Nevertheless, he maintained some furnishings at the rectory house in Colwall, perhaps to make occasional visits to the parish more comfortable, and he bequeathed a pair of vestments worth 52s. 4d. to the parish church.[42] Viall's curate in 1525 was John Joldwyn.[43] The church house was constructed on the perimeter of the churchyard to provide a focal point for parochial life c.1531,[44] a similar date and construction as the church house in the neighbouring parish of Cradley.[45] At the end of Henry VIII's reign the parish was served by the curate Thomas Taylor.[46] No chantries were then established in the parish, but in 1547 four tapers were maintained before the high altar.[47] In 1553 the church possessed a chalice and paten of silver parcel gilt, weighing 8 oz., and four bells hung in its tower.[48]

Colwall was the setting for two Puritan tracts dating from the early 17th century. In a pamphlet published in 1600, the unfortunate details of a 'monstrous birth' that had taken place in the parish were used to admonish those guilty of 'incest and whoredom'.[49] The detailed account of events in the parish, including the baptism of the child under the name 'What-God-Will', suggests that the author's correspondent was local. Another depiction of Colwall, found in an unpublished manuscript poem written between 1600 and 1615, describes the traditional entertainments by which the parishioners 'profaned' the Sabbath, including carousing in the church house between services, feasting, dancing around May poles, and playing games.[50] The author dismissed the clergyman at Colwall, presumably Richard Barnard alias Nicholas (rector from 1575), as 'illiterate, unfit to guide and teach his people'.[51] Barnard was said to have been a poor man employed in the household of Bishop Scory and who was not ordained when he was collated. Unlike previous incumbents, Barnard held no other benefices and resided in Colwall. In 1607 he complained that he was left impoverished by a lease of the rectory estate made by his predecessor Henry Tanner, who had been presented to a prebend one month after he has made the lease to the bishop's son. Barnard's straitened circumstances forced him to make a living by brewing malt.[52]

42   TNA, PROB 11/22/234.
43   *Reg. Bothe*, 171.
44   D. James, 'Buildings, 2014', *TWNFC*, 62 (2014), 169–71; Brooks and Pevsner, *Herefs.* 176; NHLE, no. 1302409, The Church Cottage (accessed 30 Sept. 2019); HAS, AR96.
45   D. James, 'Buildings, 2014', *TWNFC*, 62 (2014), 170–1; NHLE, no. 1082300, Parish Hall (accessed 4 Oct. 2019); D.W.H. Miles and M.J. Worthington, 'The tree-ring dating of Cradley Village Hall, Cradley, Herefs', Historic England Research Reports, 10/2004.
46   HAS, 32/2/1, will of Anne Ockey 1545; 23/1/3, will of Richard Hooper 1545.
47   TNA, E 301/24–6; HAS, 6/5/14, will of John Barrett, 1547.
48   TNA, E 117/2/87.
49   [Richard Jones], *A most straunge, and true discourse, of the wonderfull iudgement of God* (1600), copy available at HAS, pamp. 580.
50   BL, Add. MS 14826, f. 96; above, Social History.
51   BL, Add. MS 14826, f. 96v.
52   TNA, C 2/JasI/B19/71.

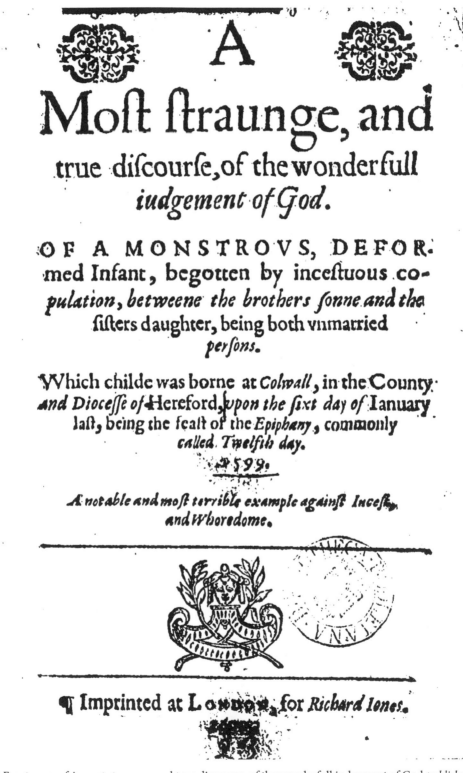

A

Moſt ſtraunge, and

true diſcourſe, of the wonderfull
iudgement of God.

OF A MONSTROVS, DEFOR-
med Infant, begotten by inceſtuous co-
pulation, betweene the brothers ſonne and the
ſiſters daughter, being both vnmarried
perſons.

Which childe was borne at Colwall, in the County
and Dioceſſe of Hereford, vpon the ſixt day of Ianuary
laſt, being the feaſt of the Epiphany, commonly
called. Twelfth day.
1599.

A notable and moſt terrible example againſt Inceſt,
and Whoredome.

¶ Imprinted at London, for Richard Iones.

Figure 25 *Front cover of* A most straunge, and true discourse, of the wonderfull iudgement of God *published in 1600 by Richard Jones.*

1640–1840s

Barnard's successor John Haylings, who may have been present in the parish by 1623,[53] was described as a preaching minister in 1656,[54] when it was recommended that Eastnor should be united to Colwall.[55] Haylings was also master at the grammar school, as was his successor John Page, suggesting both lived in the parish.[56] Page was also the rector of Coddington, the first of several incumbents to hold both parishes together. The absentee Thomas Hensleigh,[57] who held three other parishes in Berkshire and Shropshire,[58] employed Thomas Biddulph as his curate in 1759, with a salary of £30 a year.[59] Uvedale Kyffin, another non-resident pluralist, employed William Reece, the vicar of Bosbury and rector of Coddington, as his curate at Colwall.[60] Reece was himself collated to the rectory of Colwall in 1777, when he resigned his other livings.[61] After his death in 1781 he was succeeded by Joseph Taylor, who also resigned Coddington upon his appointment to Colwall.[62] James Charles Clarke, rector 1789–1831, employed a number of curates. James Barrett was employed with a stipend of £35 in 1789,[63] George Wallett with £50 in 1804,[64] and John Pearce Hockin with £75 in 1820.[65] Hockin, who had been rector of Coddington since 1810, served as curate at Colwall until 1828,[66] when he was dismissed for having caused the dissatisfaction of his congregation. A relative of the bishop, he was said to have lived in 'beggary, drunkenness and infamy'.[67]

Hockin was replaced by Thomas Dean, 'a resident clergyman of great respectability… who was beloved by his flock and respected by his neighbours'.[68] Dean was also headmaster of the grammar school. Fears that Dean was to be replaced in 1831 upon the collation of a new rector were unfounded, and his stipend was raised from £80 a year to £120.[69] In January 1833 he preached at Ledbury in support of the National Society for Promoting the Education of the Poor. He was a founder member and active supporter of the Ledbury Friendly Assurance Society.[70] To improve attendance at the parish church, Dean obtained a grant from the Incorporated Church Building Society in 1837 to re-pew the church.[71] Thirty new pews provided an extra 150 free sittings, while a new west

53   HAS, 33/2/52, will of John Rowberry, 1623.
54   LPL, COMM.XIIa/10, f. 3.
55   LPL, COMM.XIIa/10, f. 8v.
56   *CCED*, no. 173040.
57   *Heref. Institutions*, 86.
58   *CCED*, no. 68643; *Alumni Oxon. 1715–1886*, 647.
59   *CCED*, no. 102923.
60   *CCED*, no. 173621.
61   *Heref. Institutions*, 109.
62   *Heref. Institutions*, 113; *CCED*, no. 174090.
63   *CCED*, no. 102737.
64   *CCED*, no.174328.
65   *CCED*, no. 171814.
66   *CCED*, no. 105753; *Alumni Oxon. 1715–1886*, 670.
67   *Heref. Jnl*, 23 Nov. 1831; A.L. Moir, *Bishops of Heref.* (Heref. 1964), 60.
68   *Heref. Jnl*, 30 Nov. 1831; 7 Dec. 1831; 21 Dec. 1831.
69   *CCED*, no. 104385.
70   *Heref. Jnl*, 23 Jan. 1833; 3 May 1836; 1 Aug. 1838; 22 Aug. 1832; 16 Aug. 1836.
71   HAS, HD8/12; LPL, ICBS 2183.

gallery provided accommodation to pupils of the grammar school, although several large private pews remained after the work was completed in 1838.[72]

Since 1841

The revival of church life initiated by Dean continued during the 26-year incumbency of Frederick Custance, who resided at Colwall as rector of the parish from 1841 until his death in 1867.[73] At his instigation, a new rectory house was erected soon after his arrival in the parish.[74] He established a Sunday school in 1850, and presided over two services on Sundays in the parish church. On the morning of Census Sunday 1851, the parish church had an attendance of 196, including 48 Sunday school pupils, and 95 attended in the afternoon, including 37 Sunday scholars.[75] Custance was interested in improving the educational opportunities within the parish, and he provided popular free fortnightly lectures on secular subjects from 1854 until the day of his death.[76] In 1856 a National school was built at the Wyche which also served as a chapel of ease for Upper Colwall, where Custance held services twice a week.[77] At the parish church Custance introduced a choir which was acknowledged to be one of the best in the county, trained by his two daughters,[78] and he represented the district on the committee of the Herefordshire Choral Union.[79] Custance was keen to undertake the restoration of the church, but was successfully opposed by Henry Bright, whose tenants comprised a majority at a vestry held in 1863.[80] Despite this, the rector had the 'very plain' chancel completely rebuilt in a more ornamental style at his own expense in 1865–6, with a stone reredos, timber chancel screen, and a new organ.[81] He was also instrumental in the erection of a large new girls' school at Colwall Green in 1866.[82]

Custance was succeeded in 1867 by his curate and son, George Musgrave Custance.[83] A member of the Society of the Holy Cross, his introduction of Anglo-Catholic doctrines, in particular the practice of confession, caused some controversy within the district.[84] In 1878 he supported the establishment of a branch of the Oddfellows Friendly Society in Colwall.[85] In 1879 his 'appropriate sermons' and the 'precision and effect by the choir' of the parish drew approval from the surrounding district.[86] A major restoration and enlargement of the church was undertaken in 1880–1, when the west gallery was removed and a new north aisle was constructed, providing accommodation for 344.[87]

72   HAS, CK23/44, pp. 343–4, 352, 358–9, 366.
73   *Heref. Institutions*, 157; *Heref. Jnl*, 6 Apr. 1867, 8.
74   Above, Rectory House.
75   TNA, HO 129/346; HAS, X107.
76   *Heref. Jnl*, 6 Apr. 1867.
77   CERC, NS/7/1/3383; CVS, B/156; *Heref. Jnl*, 6 Apr. 1867.
78   *Heref. Times*, 12 Oct. 1861
79   A. Malpas, 'Herefs. Choral Union', *Hymns Ancient & Modern and Henry Williams Baker* (Leominster, 2013), 149.
80   *Heref. Jnl*, 12 Dec. 1863.
81   Brooks and Pevsner, *Herefs.* 176; *Heref. Jnl*, 24 Mar. 1866.
82   *Heref. Jnl*, 6 Apr. 1867.
83   *Heref. Institutions*, 180.
84   *Malvern Advertiser*, 7 July 1877; 28 July 1877; 25 Aug. 1877.
85   *Heref. Times*, 8 June 1878; *Worc. Jnl*, 5 July 1879.
86   *Worc. Jnl*, 27 Nov. 1879; 22 Feb. 1879.
87   HAS, HD10/49; LPL, ICBS 8506.

The church at the Hill School in Upper Colwall, known by this time as the Church of the Good Shepherd, had developed a distinct congregation.[88] The opening of All Saints church at Upper Wyche in Great Malvern in 1903 may have attracted some worshippers from Upper Colwall,[89] but did not apparently threaten the future of the Good Shepherd. A parishioner bequeathed three houses to establish a perpetual curacy at the church in 1906.[90] This encouraged the congregation to raise funds for the erection of a new building, constructed between 1908 and 1910 on a plot next to the school in a 'free Perpendicular style with Art Nouveau touches'.[91]

Custance resigned the rectory in 1902, to be replaced by Frederick William Carnegy.[92] Charles Harris, rector 1909–29, is remembered for having set Sir John Stanhope Arkwright's poem 'The Supreme Sacrifice' to music, as the hymn 'O Valiant Hearts'.[93] First performed at Colwall to commemorate Harris's son, killed in 1917, it was performed before the king later that year at Westminster Abbey, and at the dedication of the Tomb of the Unknown Warrior in 1920.[94] Sales of the composition supported the construction of the parish war memorial, erected in the garden of the rectory in 1920.[95] During his incumbency, the congregation of the Good Shepherd continued to grow, having its own churchwardens and vestry by the 1920s,[96] and the curate's stipend was augmented in 1925.[97] A second chapel of ease, St. Crispin's, was built in Mill Lane in 1927, adjoining the Church Rooms erected at the same time.

Harris was replaced as rector by Ernest Maitland Cooke in 1930.[98] Cooke was succeeded in turn by George Victor Sumner, rector between 1936 and 1938. In 1931 there were 350 seats at the parish church, 200 at the Good Shepherd, and 50 at St Crispin's.[99] A total of 400 congregants attended Easter services in 1933, 246 at the parish church and 154 at the Good Shepherd.[100] A chapel at Evendine, presumably a private one in the domestic service college, contained 15 seats.[101] The expense of building the Good Shepherd diminished the endowment of the curacy, and in 1934 a proposal was considered to set aside £1,000 for the curate. A surplus in the curates' fund was later set aside to pay for a curate's house.[102] Arthur Cecil White, rector 1938–49, left a diary for 1943–6 which records the spiritual life of the parish, Colwall's experience of the Second World War, and his struggles to maintain his garden.[103] In 1944 there were four services a day on Sundays, divided equally between the parish church and the Good Shepherd.

88   *Worc. Jnl,* 22 Oct. 1881.
89   *VCH Worcs.* IV, 132.
90   HAS, CK23/45, 16 Apr. 1906, 23 Mar. 1907.
91   Brooks and Pevsner, *Herefs.* 179; HAS, T17/1; R95/22/26.
92   *Alumni Cantab.* 1752–1900, I, 516.
93   *Crockford's Clerical Dir.* (1932), 568; Weaver, *Herefs. Biography,* 197; Ballard, *Colwall Collection,* 69–71.
94   *Herefs. Times,* 21 July 1917; *The Times,* 3 Aug. 1917; *Kington Times,* 13 Nov. 1920.
95   NHLE, no. 1461608, Colwall War Memorial (accessed 30 Sep. 2019). Below, Church Architecture.
96   HAS, CK23/46.
97   Above, Parish Origins and Parochial Organisation.
98   *Crockford's Clerical Dir.* (1932), 268.
99   HAS, CK23/46; AK78/8.
100 HAS, AK78/1.
101 HAS, CK23/46; AK78/8.
102 HAS, AK78/4.
103 HAS, CK23/43.

Figure 26
*Photograph of
Colwall Green
Methodist
Chapel.*

After White's death in 1949, L. Andrew Whatley was appointed to the rectory, succeeded in 1963 by Harry Whatley. From 1978 services alternated each week between the parish church and the Good Shepherd.[104] The benefice was united with Coddington in 1982, but the new rector, Carl Attwood, remained resident in Colwall.[105] The Good Shepherd closed in 1992, and was converted to social housing in 1994. The Chancel was retained as a church room.[106] Attwood retired in 2008, and was replaced by Melanie Horton, the parish's first female rector.[107] In 2019 there are services every Sunday at the parish church, and services at St Crispin's on three Sundays each month; weekly evening services alternate between St Crispin's and the rectory.[108]

Nonconformity and Roman Catholicism

There was little support for Nonconformity in the parish in the late 17th century. Although John Barston (d. 1701), the ejected former rector of Aylton, was licensed to hold meetings at his house in Colwall in 1672,[109] four years later the Compton census recorded only two Nonconformists in the parish. No Catholics were reported in 1676,[110] and only one Catholic in 1767.[111] Five Nonconformist meeting houses were licensed

---

104 *Colwall Clock*, Sept. 1992.
105 Inf. from Susan Lawson, assistant to the Bp. of Heref; *Malvern Gaz.*, 20 Mar. 2008.
106 *Colwall Clock*, Sep. 1992; Dec. 1994.
107 *Malvern Gaz.*, 20 Mar. 2008; 19 Aug. 2008.
108 'Colwall with Upper Colwall', https://www.achurchnearyou.com/church/10482/service-and-events/events-regular (accessed 26 Mar. 2019).
109 *Calamy Revised*, ed. A.G. Matthews (Oxford, 1988), 31.
110 *Compton Census*, ed. A. Whiteman (1986), 260.
111 HAS, HD2/16/33.

in Colwall between 1827 and 1836.[112] Despite the number of licences issued, the congregations were small, and initially struggled to establish themselves.

A Baptist meeting was licensed in 1834 at the house in Broadfield occupied by George Henry Roper Curzon,[113] who had previously founded a meeting at Ledbury after his rejection as too enthusiastic for ordination in the Church of England.[114] The house in Colwall was presumably Teynham House in Upper Colwall, where a chapel was recorded in 1842.[115] However Curzon had moved away by 1842, and the congregation appears to have dissolved without his influence. By 1851 his house had reverted to a private residence.[116]

A small congregation of c.25 Wesleyan Methodists met in 1851 for services in the afternoons and evenings, at a private residence in the parish, perhaps one of those licensed for worship earlier in the century.[117] In 1858 they erected a small chapel, comprising a single room, at the corner of Colwall Green.[118] A second congregation of Wesleyan Methodists was reported at the Wyche in 1863, but there is no further record of the group.[119] The chapel at Colwall Green was extended in the 1940s with the addition of a room for its Sunday school.[120] It was closed in 2004, and the building converted for residential use.[121]

The Congregationalist mission chapel was erected at the Wyche in 1856 by a group associated with the Congregationalist chapel in Malvern.[122] The mission chapel was adopted by the Malvern chapel as one of its four village stations by 1875. A room at the rear of the chapel was utilised for a Sunday school until 1904, and the chapel continued in use until at least 1908, but had certainly closed by 1916.[123] A distinct chapel, called the Wyche Free Church, was constructed nearby and opened in 1911. Although there were connections between its early trustees and the mission chapel, the new Free church was intended to be an independent and non-denominational place of worship.[124] Designed by Harold Seymour Scott, best known for his work on early art-deco cinemas, it is built in a Voysey-esque style, with rendered walls, a slate roof and angled buttresses, a hipped porch at the south-west corner, and a polygonal apse at the north end.[125] In 1919 the trustees of the Free Church purchased the defunct Congregationalist mission

112 HAS, CA19/1, 2, 3; HD8/11a.
113 HAS, CA19/3, HD7; *Complete Peerage*, ed. G. White (1953), XII, 688.
114 Brooks and Pevsner, *Herefs.* 420; footnote reference to Baptist Handbook, 1862; *Pigot's Dir.* (1830, 1835 edns).
115 HAS, CA19/3, HD8; AL59/1; M5/44/17.
116 HAS, HD8/11a; X107; M5/6/67.
117 TNA, HO 129/346; HAS, X107.
118 HAS, AL 29/11; Brooks and Pevsner, *Herefs.* 177; HER, 35670.
119 T. Marsh, research on Colwall, Colwall Society cupboard, Colwall Library; *Kelly's Dir.* (1885, 1891, 1909 edns); *Jakeman and Carver Dir. and Gaz. for Herefs.* (1890). Later references to a Methodist chapel at the Wyche are probably an error for the Congregationalist chapel.
120 M. Ritchie, *Now and Then*; HAS, AL29/11.
121 M. Ritchie, *Now and Then*; Sale particulars for chapel, 2007, John Goodwin, Estate Agent, Ledbury.
122 Goodbury, *Light on the Hill*, 3.
123 Ibid., 9, 11; Holly Mount Congregational Chapel, Deacons' Meeting Minutes 1916–32, DM3.
124 K.C. Gaines, *Wyche Free Church* (n.d.); Goodbury, *Light on the Hill*, 13–7; Ballard, *Colwall Collection*, 52; Ellis, *Dissenters All*, 74.
125 Brooks and Pevsner, *Herefs.* 180.

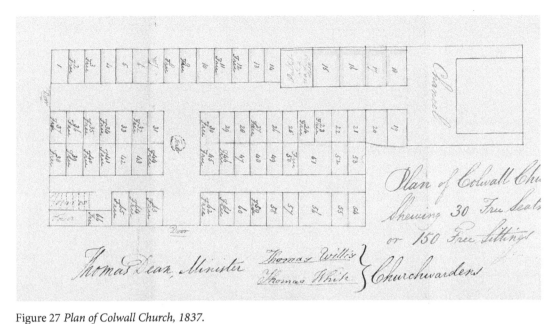

Figure 27 *Plan of Colwall Church, 1837.*

Figure 28 *Colwall parish church in 1846, by Charles F. Walker.*

chapel, which was demolished in 1923.[126] Services at the Free Church were well-attended in the 1920s, but thereafter the fortunes of the chapel fluctuated.[127] Nevertheless the congregation continued to meet, and in 2019 it was a member of the Fellowship of

126 Goodbury, *Light on the Hill*, 9, 11; Holly Mount Congregational Chapel, Deacons' Meeting Minutes 1916–32, DM3.
127 Goodbury, *Light on the Hill*, 11, 12, 28; Holly Mount Congregational Chapel, Deacons' Meeting Minutes 1930–50, DM4; *Wyche Report*, 5 (1979).

Independent Evangelical Churches, with morning and evening services every Sunday, although there was no settled minister.[128]

A meeting of the Plymouth Brethren was established in Colwall in 1839, led by a preacher from Hereford, but it relocated to Malvern in 1841.[129] Meetings recommenced before 1888, when a brick chapel was erected for them at Colwall Stone.[130] The land in Walwyn Road, purchased from the Ballards, was sold back to the family in 1891, who used the building for charitable and other social purposes, including meetings of the Band of Hope, although the Brethren continued to meet there until the 1930s. A Sunday school was established there in 1945 by two members of the Baptist church at Malvern. Baptist services later commenced in the building, which was purchased by trustees in 1966, and later renamed the Colwall Community Church.[131] The congregation of the Community Church, numbering c.60 in 2019, is too large to meet in the church building, and morning services are held every Sunday in Colwall primary school.[132]

Church Architecture

The church of St James the Great was built in the 12th century,[133] although the incorporation of an 11th-century window in the west wall may indicate it replaced an earlier church on the same site. Enlarged in the 13th and 14th centuries, and restored and enlarged in the 19th century, the present church, built of local sandstone and roofed in tile, comprises a three-bay chancel, a five-bay nave with north and south aisles, and a south-west tower.

The 12th-century doorway was reset and flanked by a pair of trumpet-scallop capitals when the south aisle was constructed in the 13th century. Construction of the three-stage tower at the south-west corner of the church began in the middle of the 14th century, the final battlemented stage completed later that century. The three mutilated niches in the east wall of the lowest stage of the tower may once have contained a statue of the Calvary, removed at the Reformation. The double-collar nave roof may also date from the late 14th century, when the west window was inserted in the nave. The timber-framed south porch dates from the 16th or 17th century. An inserted tie beam, dated 1675 with the initials of the churchwardens, suggests that significant restoration of the roof was necessary.

A more significant restoration in 1865–6 was undertaken by the architect Henry Woodyer. The chancel, 'a very plain ediface', was completely rebuilt, including the removal of two 12th-century windows,[134] and a vestry was added in an Early English

128 http://www.wychefreechurch.org.uk (accessed 26 Mar. 2019).

129 HAS, Uncatalogued minutes of the Barton Street Meeting; H.H. Rowdon, *The Origins of the Brethren* (1967), 165; T. Grass, *Gathering to His Name* (2006), 51–2.

130 Inf. from R. Eames; HER, 31907.

131 *Jakeman and Carver, Dir. and Gaz. for Herefs.* (1890); inf. from Miss E. Hawker of Malvern, and Mr. R. Eames; Ballard, *Colwall Collection*; Ellis, *Dissenters All*; S.W. Stringer, *History of Colwall* (1955).

132 *Colwall Community Church*, http://www.colwallcommunitychurch.com (accessed 26 Mar. 2019).

133 Except where otherwise stated, this account is based on RCHME, *Inventory*, II, 52–3; Brooks and Pevsner, *Herefs.* 176; NHLE, no. 1178404, Ch. of St James (accessed 30 Sept. 2019); HER, 4824; HAS, AK78/8; A. Bright, *Colwall Church: An Historical Sketch* (c.1930).

134 *Heref. Jnl*, 24 Mar. 1866; *Herefs. Churches Through Victorian Eyes: Sir Stephen Glynne's Church Notes for Herefs. with Water-colours by Charles F. Walker*, ed. J. Leonard (Little Logaston, 2006), 24.

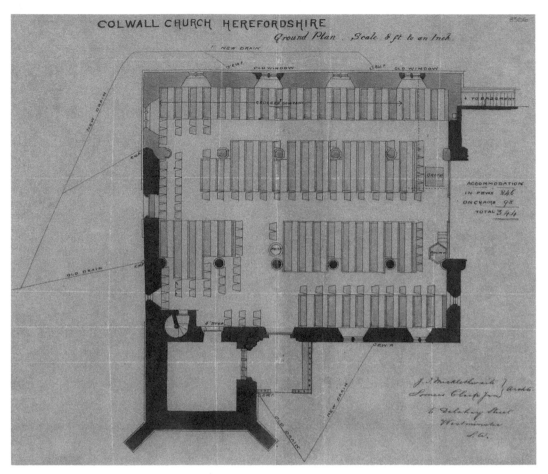

Figure 29 (above) *Ground plan of Colwall church by J.T. Micklethwaite and Somers Clarke junior, 1880–1.*

Figure 30 (left) *Photograph of Colwall church from the south-east in 2019.*

Figure 31 *Churchyard cross.*

style. Woodyer installed a new reredos of Caen stone, a timber chancel screen, a credence table, and an organ loft.[135] The church was further enlarged in 1880, when a north aisle was added by the architects John Thomas Micklethwaite and Somers Clarke, incorporating two reset 14th-century windows.[136] Woodyer's chancel screen was replaced in 1906, and later moved to the west end of the nave.[137]

A monument dated 1587, to the parents of Humphrey Walwyn, has caused the east end of the south aisle to be referred to sometimes as the Walwyn chapel. On the south wall is a brass plaque to Elizabeth Harford (d. 1590), depicting her husband Anthony and their ten children. An 18th-century stone tablet commemorates members of the Brydges family of Old Colwall. In the 18th century, the interior of the church contained six large

135 Brooks and Pevsner, *Herefs.* 176; *ODNB*, s.v. Woodyer, Henry, architect (accessed 30 Sept. 2019).
136 HAS, HD10/49.
137 HAS, HD10/88.

private pews, three on the north wall between the pulpit and the chancel, which were reconstructed in 1729.[138] The church was re-pewed *c*.1837 to provide 150 free sittings for the poor,[139] and a large west gallery was constructed to accommodate children from the grammar school. The accommodation within the church was increased further in 1873, when the box pews were replaced with open stalls.[140] The west gallery was removed in 1881, and the grammar school children were moved to pews marked 'Grocers' School' in the new north aisle. The new arrangements provided total accommodation within the church for 344, 246 in pews and 98 on chairs.[141] At the same time, Micklethwaite removed the nave ceiling to reveal the archbraces and windbraces of the roof, and rescued the early-17th-century pulpit removed by Woodyer in 1866. The font, perhaps 13th-century, has been recut and stood on a modern base.[142] The arms of Queen Anne hang in the north aisle. There are fragments of 14th- and 15th-century glass in the aisles, and 19th-century glass by Hardman in the chancel and by Kempe in the aisles.

The ring of six bells, cast by Thomas Rudhall of Gloucester in 1778, was augmented by the addition of two trebles in 1896. Another two small bells were added in 1998, and the bells of 1896 were replaced in 1999 with two more bells. A small bell, cast for the parish by Abraham Rudhall I of Gloucester in 1709, is now disused.[143]

In the churchyard stands the stump of a 15th-century cross, with the distinctive Herefordshire feature of a niche in the west face of its base.[144] The churchyard was extended in 1866 with the addition of land to the north of the church, granted to the parish by the Ecclesiastical Commissioners.[145] The churchyard was extended once more in 1897.[146] A war memorial, comprising an octagonal stone Calvary cross with a pitched roof, was erected in 1920 on part of the rectory garden adjacent to the churchyard.[147]

138 HAS, AA26/II/51.

139 Above, religious life 1640–1840.

140 *Worc. Jnl*, 4 Oct. 1873.

141 LPL, ICBS 8506.

142 G. Marshall, *Fonts in Herefs.* (*Heref.* 1951), 51.

143 F. Sharpe, *The Church Bells of Herefs.* (Brackley, 1966), 110–1; *The Ringing World*, 14 Aug. 1998, 789; 20 Aug. 1999, 796; inf. from John Eisel and Robin Riches.

144 HER, 3835; B.J. Marples, 'The niche in medieval churchyard crosses', *TWNFC* (1972), 321–3; Brooks and Pevsner, *Herefs.* 176; NHLE, no. 1349729, Churchyard Cross (accessed 30 Sept. 2019); Herefs. Libraries, AW 189, p. 190.

145 HAS, HD10/24.

146 HAS, HD10/76.

147 The War Memorial Register, http://www.iwm.org.uk/memorials/item/memorial/627 (accessed 26 Mar. 2019); NHLE, no. 1461608, Colwall War Memorial (accessed 30 Sept. 2019); HAS, T17/1; BN39/42.

LOCAL GOVERNMENT

THE PARISH OF COLWALL LAY within Radlow hundred. Colwall was one of 22 parishes and townships which formed the Ledbury poor-law union in 1836, and it joined the Ledbury highway district in 1863. It was part of Ledbury rural sanitary district from 1872, which became Ledbury rural district in 1894, when a parish council was formed for Colwall. Following the creation of Hereford and Worcester county in 1974, Colwall was placed in Malvern Hills district council. From 1976 Colwall together with Coddington, Mathon and Wellington Heath formed Hope End ward of Malvern Council.[1] Since 1998 Colwall has been part of Herefordshire council.

Manorial Government

By at least the late 15th century Colwall was considered a parcel of the manor of Bosbury, where tenants attended the bishop's court.[2] The manor of Barton Colwall dealt primarily with conveyances of property and encroachments upon the waste. Although Brockbury was reputed a manor, no records of its courts survive.[3]

Bosbury, Colwall and Coddington

Although apparently originally a distinct manor, by the late middle ages the bishop's tenants did suit and service at his court of Bosbury.[4] Court rolls and manorial accounts are extant from the late 15th century. From 1661 to the early 20th century records of the courts are preserved in a series of court books.[5] Routine business of the court included admissions and surrenders, stray animals, encroachments, repairs to dilapidated tenements and deteriorated highways, and the appointment of a constable. The twice-yearly courts with view of frankpledge also dealt with minor civil pleas including breaches of the assizes of bread and ale, nuisances and disputes.

A woman was presented as a common brewer in 1476.[6] Richard Hartland was amerced over £5 for performing a rescue upon the lord's bailiff and diverse other offences c.1592, while Richard Hall of Worcester was amerced for not residing upon his customary land within the manor.[7] In 1619 the jurors presented three men for keeping

1   HAS, CG36/2, p. 84.
2   *VCH Herefs. Bosbury*, 27–8.
3   Only a map survives for Brockbury manor: HAS, AT51; MF General X165.
4   HAS, AM33/1–2, 6, 8–9, 13–7; AA59/A/2; BL, Add. Roll 27311; Add. Ch. 27245; TNA, SC 6/HENVIII/1511.
5   HAS, AA63/1–38.
6   HAS, AM33/1.
7   HAS, AM33/16.

alehouses, and one man for taking in inmates into his cottage. A man was presented for encroaching upon the common pasture called '*Veldiat*' with his cattle, and another for overloading the commons with his sheep. The inhabitants were ordered to ring and yoke their pigs, and two men were required to remove their goats from the manor. The archery butts were out of repair.[8]

During the late 17th century the courts largely dealt with admissions and surrenders, maintenance of watercourses, boundaries, and roads and the appointment of constables, although the jurors also presented individuals for building cottages upon the waste, and for taking in lodgers.[9] By the 18th century the bishop's court was solely concerned with administration of customary tenure (recording the transfer of copyholds) on the manor. Books and minute books regarding copyhold business cover the years 1787–1859.[10] The court continued to meet twice a year until 1875, then annually until the final court in 1896,[11] although court business continued to be transacted out of court until 1943. Many of the later court books also deal with the abolition of copyholds and the extinguishment of manorial incidents as a number of tenants enfranchised their copyhold property between 1852–66, and again between 1918–22.[12]

Barton Colwall

No medieval court records have been traced for Barton Colwall, but extant deeds from the 16th century indicate that courts were being held in the 16th and 17th centuries.[13] A survey of the manor was recorded in 1719,[14] and terriers of the manor were produced in the late 18th century.[15] Court books from 1716 until 1885 deal predominantly with admissions and surrenders.[16] There was no pound in 1746.[17] Encroachments upon Brand Green, Colwall Green, and Gardener's Common were presented in the late 18th century.[18] A survey of encroachments upon the commons since 1793 was made c.1834.[19] From 1811 meetings only took place when there was business to transact.[20] Encroachments upon Colwall Green, including by the West Midland Railway, were recorded in 1861–2.[21]

Parochial Government until 1894

The parish was served by two churchwardens by the early 17th century, and subsequently, although only one churchwarden was appointed in 1846.[22] A vestry

8   HAS, AM33/8.
9   HAS, AA63/1–7.
10   HAS, AA63/40–2, 44.
11   HAS, AA63/36.
12   TNA, MAF 9/110/29–47; MAF 20/21.
13   HAS, AE30/435–7.
14   HAS, AA26/I/6–8, AA26/III/4; AE32/1
15   HAS, AA26/III/7–9.
16   HAS, AA26/I/1–3.
17   HAS, AA26/IV/6.
18   HAS, AA26/IV/6–7.
19   HAS, AE30/530.
20   HAS, AA26/1/2–3.
21   HAS, AA26/1/2.
22   HAS, HD2/1/28; AE30/423; CL23/44.

appears to have existed by 1764,[23] and minutes are extant from 1801 to 1887.[24] Until 1806 meetings were usually held at the rectory; between that year and 1817 they were usually held at the Horse & Groom inn, when they moved to the parish church. From 1844 until 1879 meetings were held either at the church or at the girls' schoolroom, after which the vestry usually met at the free school at Colwall Green.

In the 18th and 19th centuries, the parish appointed two constables, two overseers, and two surveyors of the highways, reduced to one surveyor from 1835.[25] As well as the paid constables, by 1852 a number of other constables were named to serve as unpaid constables to look after parts of the parish.[26] Following the creation of the Ledbury highway district in 1863 a waywarden was appointed for the parish.[27] In 1882 the district was divided between two surveyors, each having responsibility for some Colwall roads.[28] The highway district was superseded by the Ledbury rural district in 1894.

Poor Law Administration

There are poor rate assessments and overseers' accounts for the years 1720, 1732–3, and 1764.[29] In 1732–3 a total of £18 15s. 4d. was disbursed, mostly on out-relief.[30] Money was also expended in minor repairs upon the church house. The estimated weekly cost of relief was 11s. 7d. in 1759.[31] In the three years ending Easter 1785 an average of c.£196 was spent by the overseers; by 1802–3 this had risen to almost £346, of which c.£306 was spent upon maintenance and relief.[32] In that year 37 individuals received out-relief permanently and 36 occasionally, of whom 11 were elderly or too infirm to work. From 1803 the parish made payments for the apprenticing of poor children, who were selected by lot or ticket.[33] In the year 1813–4 expenditure upon poor relief amounted to £545, which fell to £348 in the following year.[34] A total of 28 individuals were permanently in receipt of poor relief; in 1813–4 50 people also received relief occasionally, rising to 60 in the following year. An assistant overseer was appointed in 1823 with a salary of £15.[35] Expenditure on relief was c.£282 in 1826–7, fell to c.£184 in 1829–30, and subsequently rose to £404 in 1833–4.[36] In the year ending Easter 1835 the parish spent c.£229 on maintaining the poor, a figure which fell to c.£194 in the following year.[37] In May 1740 the overseers agreed to purchase a cottage and land,[38] and by 1836 the parish owned 11 dwellings. In one cottage the occupier paid the overseers the full rent, but the remainder

23   HAS, AE30/423.
24   HAS, CK23/44.
25   HAS, AE30/423–4; CK23/44.
26   HAS, CK23/44, p. 451.
27   HAS, CK23/44, p. 520; K41/1.
28   HAS, K41/2, p. 173.
29   HAS, AE30/422–4.
30   HAS, AE30/424.
31   HAS, AE30/425.
32   *Poor Law Abstract, 1804* (Parl. Papers, 1804 (175), i), pp. 192–3.
33   HAS, CK23/44, pp. 79, 218.
34   *Poor Law Abstract, 1818* (Parl. Papers, 1818 (82), xix), pp. 164–5.
35   HAS, CK23/44, p. 239.
36   *Poor Law Returns, 1825–9* (Parl. Papers, 1830–1 (83), xi), p. 74; *Poor Law Returns, 1830–4* (Parl. Papers, 1835 (444), xlvii), p. 73.
37   *Poor Law Com. 2nd Rep.* (Parl. Papers, 1836 (595), xxix (1)), Appendix D, pp. 132–3.
38   Eastnor Castle Archive, Colwall deeds box (second bundle).

were occupied by families at reduced or no rent, some of whom also received relief from the parish.[39]

After its inclusion in Ledbury poor-law union in 1836, Colwall elected one guardian,[40] and lands belonging to the parish for the support of the poor were sold.[41] A proposal to transfer Colwall to Malvern union was rejected by the parish in 1870.[42] The number of guardians elected by the parish was increased to two in 1885.[43] The union workhouse, opened in 1837, was at Ledbury;[44] in 1851 three inmates were from Colwall,[45] and in 1893–4 nine parishioners were at the workhouse.[46]

Local Government since 1894

Ledbury Rural District Council

Colwall elected three representatives to the district council, increasing to six in 1938.[47] A parochial committee was established in 1895, comprising parish councillors and one district councillor, which met monthly until 1955 to manage sewerage and refuse collection, housing, water pollution, enforcement of bye-laws, notification of infectious diseases, and planning applications.[48] Meetings were initially held at the Temperance Hall, but later moved to the Workmen's Hall and the Temperance Hotel, settling upon the council room in 1923. T. A. Pedlingham served as chairman from at least 1914 until his death in 1938,[49] while Ewart Ballard was also a prominent member who served as councillor 1946–69.[50]

The parish council was appointed a housing committee by the district council in 1913 to build workmen's cottages. A piece of land near Lugg's Mill farm was selected for the construction of eight cottages but the scheme was abandoned in 1915.[51] Refuse collection in the parish started in December 1928.[52] Proposals to grant Colwall urban powers were rejected by the Ministry of Health c.1933.[53] Renewed efforts by the county council in 1935 and 1937 were again defeated after an appeal by the district council and a local enquiry.[54] Colwall was placed within the district of Malvern Fire Brigade in 1939.[55] Colwall was attached to Malvern Urban District Council for water powers in 1958.[56]

39   HAS, K42/342, 16 Aug. 1836.
40   HAS, K42/342, p. 1; F. Youngs, *Local Admin. Units: Northern England* (1991), 126.
41   HAS, CK23/44, p. 348; above, Social History.
42   HAS, CK23/44, p. 511.
43   HAS, K42/364, p. 131.
44   HAS, K42/342–74.
45   HAS, X7/1.
46   HAS, T9/28–31.
47   HAS, BW15/13/2, pp. 41, 61.
48   HAS, AG79/1, p. 21; BW15/13/4, p. 129; T9/58–62.
49   HAS, T9/59–62.
50   HAS, BW15/13/2–4
51   HAS, T9/51–53.
52   HAS, T9/61.
53   HAS, BW15/13/1, pp. 167, 186.
54   HAS, BW15/13/1, pp. 373, 386–7; BW15/13/2, pp. 18, 28, 36.
55   HAS, BW15/13/2, p. 94.
56   HAS, CG36/1, 12 Mar. 1958.

Parish Council

In 1894 a parish council was formed, holding its first meeting at the girls' school, where Fred Ballard was elected its first chairman.[57] Between 1895 and 1899 meetings were held at the Workmen's Hall, moving to the Temperance Hotel until 1923, when the council leased a room in Stone Drive which became known as the council room.[58] Several sub-committees were established, including at various times for lighting, finance, the library, and planning and development.[59] It appointed representatives to the Malvern Hills conservators, managers for the local schools and trustees for the parochial charities.[60]

The council was primarily concerned with planning, local rates, highways, the appointment of overseers, and the administration of several parish charities.[61] Both the parish council and the district council were keen to limit housing development outside the village.[62] The council agreed a new rate for street lighting in 1897, and libraries in 1898.[63] Street lighting was introduced in 1899, and both gas and oil lamps were installed in the parish.[64] A sanitary committee was established in 1899, after councillor and local doctor Samuel McMillan identified an increase in cases of tuberculosis.[65] The council acquired a fire engine in 1900 with a loan of £300.[66] The council objected to the Malvern Water bill in 1905;[67] following the passage of the Act a dispute arose between it and Malvern Urban District Council over the purchase of land for the reservoir at Park Wood.[68]

The council managed Colwall Green and adjacent land on behalf of the Malvern Hills conservators until 1976, when responsibility for the green was vested in them directly.[69] Responsibility for street lighting was transferred to the RDC, but restored to the parish council between 1955 and 1974.[70] In 1974 council meetings moved to Colwall Park Hotel for a year before moving to the Valley school.[71] Between 1977–99 the council issued bus tokens to pensioners living in the parish.[72] The council were involved in building the new village hall, completed in 1992,[73] when it also took over responsibility for the management of Walwyn meadow and library from the Walwyn Educational Foundation.[74]

57   HAS, AG79/1.
58   HAS, AG79/1-4; AG79/4, 14 Mar. 1923.
59   HAS, CG36/1–5; T9/51–7.
60   HAS, CG36, passim.
61   HAS, T9/79; AG79/1–6.
62   HAS, CG36, passim.
63   HAS, AG79/1, pp. 86, 109.
64   HAS, T9/35–8.
65   *Worc. Chron.* 15 July 1899; 2 Sept. 1899; 11 Jan. 1902.
66   HAS, T9/79.
67   HAS, AG79/2, p. 67.
68   WAAS, 493:22 BA9581/16.
69   HAS, CG36/1, 12 Jan. 1955; CG36/2, p. 103.
70   HAS, T9/37.
71   HAS, CG36/1; CG36/2, 3 Apr. 1974; C36/2, p. 61.
72   HAS, CG36/2, p. 136; CG36/7, 4 Jan. 1999.
73   HAS, CG36/4–5.
74   HAS, CG36/4, 27 Jan. 1992.

In 1994 the council took over responsibility for the Pedlingham Clock Trust,[75] and successfully resisted attempts for responsibility for street lighting to be restored to it.[76]

The Malvern Hills Conservators

A Malvern Hills Preservation Association was formed in 1876 to protect the commons from encroachments and enclosure.[77] In 1882 a committee was formed to steer a bill through Parliament to establish conservators for the hills.[78] The first meeting of the Commoners' Committee took place at the Winnings in April 1883, attended by Stephen Ballard and Robert Raper.[79] The Malvern Hills Act was passed in 1884, appointing 15 conservators to manage a large portion of the hills, including land in Colwall. They were to prevent encroachment upon the Malvern Hills, preserve common rights, and provide recreational space for the public.[80] Under the terms of the Act two conservators were appointed by Colwall vestry, and two by the owners of estates in the parish. Robert Raper, one of the leading proponents of the conservation of the Malvern Hills, granted the conservators 16 a. of land belonging to his Hoe Court estate in 1886,[81] giving him the power to appoint a conservator from 1887.[82] Fred Ballard was elected chairman of the conservators in 1909.[83]

The conservators were empowered to raise a rate of up to ½d. in the pound in Colwall and neighbouring parishes, and the parish overseers were also required to contribute towards the costs of the work of the conservators. Despite concerns over the potential for irreparable damage to be caused to the hills by quarrying, the original Act did not extinguish the mineral rights of landowners within the parish. Many of the quarries on the Colwall side of the hills were owned by the Ecclesiastical Commissioners, and most of these were closed c.1886, leaving only Gardiner's and Wyche quarries open in Colwall.[84] The conservators took a lease of one of the quarries from the commissioners in 1887, in order to manage its output.[85] Nevertheless, they were unable to prevent quarrying without the compliance of the landowners, and Ledbury highway board opened a new quarry close to the Wyche in 1888.[86] The conservators took a ten-year lease of all of the quarries in Colwall in 1903.[87] Two years later Raper, who had purchased the manor of Barton Colwall, transferred his rights to the conservators in order to prevent future quarrying on Herefordshire Beacon.[88]

75 HAS, CG36/5, 19 Jan. 1994.
76 HAS, CG36/1–2; CG36/5, 16 Feb. 1994.
77 Hurle, *The Malvern Hills*, 20–2.
78 *Worcs. Chron.* 22 Sept. 1882; *Heref. Times*, 23 Sept. 1882; Hurle, *The Malvern Hills*, 28–9.
79 MHC minute book, 1883–4, 7 Apr. 1883.
80 47 & 48 Vic. c.clxxv.
81 MHC minute book, 1884–6, p. 138.
82 MHC minute books, 1884–6, p. 138; 1887, p. 4.
83 MHC minute book, 1899–1909, p. 273.
84 MHC minutes book, 1884–6, pp. 127, 141. Despite its name, Colwall Park Quarry was in Mathon.
85 HAS, AA26/IV/6.
86 MHC minute book, 1888–9, p. 46.
87 MHC minute book, 1899–1909, p. 114.
88 MHC minute book, 1899–1909, p. 183; HAS, AA26/II/76; AA26/IV/8.

Subsequent Acts of Parliament modified the terms of the original Act. From 1909 two of 18 conservators were to be elected by parishioners of Colwall,[89] and from 1924 one of 25 conservators was to be appointed by Colwall parish council and another two elected by Colwall inhabitants.[90] The 1924 Act also gave the conservators the power to preserve the natural conditions of the hills, and to purchase land or the common or mineral rights over it. The Act gave the Minister of Agriculture the power to prohibit quarrying upon the application of the conservators, although licenses for quarrying were still permissible for local public purposes.[91] In 1929 the conservators used their powers of compulsory purchase to acquire the manorial rights of George Ballard.[92] The Government decided in 1953 that quarrying on the Hills should be prohibited.[93] Further acts were passed in 1930 and 1995.[94] In 2017 the governing body adopted the working name of the Malvern Hills Trust, and the 29 conservators became a board of trustees.[95]

89   9 Edw. VIII c.xxxvii.
90   14 & 15 Geo. V c.xxxvi.
91   14 & 15 Geo. V c.xxxvi.
92   MHC minute book, 1928–31, p. 118.
93   Above, Economic History.
94   20 & 21 Geo. V c.lxxii; 1995 c.iii.
95   Malvern Hills Trust, 'Report of the trustees for the year ending 31st March 2017', http://www.
     malvernhills.org.uk/media/1384/malvern-hills-trust-signed-accounts-31317.pdf (accessed 28 Mar.
     2019).

THIS NOTE DISCUSSES THE MAIN manuscript and printed sources used in writing the history of Colwall. It is not comprehensive and should be used in conjunction with the List of Abbreviations. Herefordshire Archive Service, the principal archive used, is listed first, followed by other archives in alphabetical order, and the published sources, primary and secondary. The Bright Family Papers, which are held by The University of Melbourne Archives have not been consulted.

Manuscript Sources

Herefordshire Archive Service at Herefordshire Archive and Records Centre (HARC), Hereford holds the records of county government (including inclosure awards and 18th and 19th century land tax assessments), the Hereford diocesan and archidiaconal records (including bishops' registers, documents relating to the administration of the bishop's estates, and church terriers), estate and family papers and nonconformist records. It also has a large collection of private records including charters and accounts. The principal documents used in this history are:

AA26:	Barton Court Estate
AA59/A/1:	Rental of the bishop's manors, *c.*1288
AA59/A/2:	Survey of the bishop's estates by Swithun Butterfield, 1577
AA63:	Court books for the bishop's manors
AE30:	Deeds, estate and family papers of the Bright family of Colwall
AK99:	Colwall Parish Records, 1558–1991
AM33:	Bailiffs' accounts and court records for the bishop's manors, 1497–1592
HD4/1:	Court books for the diocese of Hereford
HD5, HD8, HD10:	Diocesan records, mainly relating to parish clergy and parish administration
M5:	Sale particulars
Q:	Records of Quarter Sessions, responsible for county administration from the 16th to the 19th centuries, including Q/REL (land tax assessments from 1787)

Local wills proved in the diocesan court in the 16th and 17th centuries; these are numbered in the form 9/3/46, with no preliminary letters.

British Library, London, holds numerous original deeds, manorial records, tracts, private papers, and maps, including the original drawings of the Ordnance Survey.

Colwall Library holds various local publications, including those of the Colwall Village Society.

Guildhall Library, London holds papers relating to Humphrey Walwyn's Charity and Walwyn's Free School, Colwall.

Herefordshire Historic Environment Record, Herefordshire Archive and Records Centre, Hereford (formerly the Sites and Monuments Record) holds notes of archaeological sites and features and of listed buildings. It is accessible at Herefordshire Through Time: https://htt.herefordshire.gov.uk/

Hereford Cathedral Library holds the cathedral archives including early charters and transcripts of the Chapter Act Books.

Lambeth Palace Library, London holds Incorporated Church Building Society (ICBS) plans.

The Church of England Record Centre, London holds the records of the Ecclesiastical Commissioners for England and the National Society for Promoting Religious Education.

The National Archives at Kew, London, holds the records of national government from the late 12th century onwards. Calendars of some medieval administrative records which have been used in this history, notably the Close and Patent Rolls, have been published. The classes of documents used in this history include:

C 1:	Chancery, Pleadings, Richard II to Phillip and Mary.
C 2:	Chancery: Pleadings, Series II, Elizabeth I to Charles I
CP 25:	Feet of Fines (note of agreements reached in, often fictitious, land disputes)
E 320:	Particulars for the sale of the estates of Charles I, 1649–60
HO 107:	Home Office, Census Enumerators' returns, 1841, 1851
HO 129:	Home Office, Ecclesiastical census 1851
IR 18/3010:	Tithe files, Colwall, agreement and apportionment, 1836–70
IR 29/14/52:	Tithe Commission and its Successors: Colwall tithe apportionment, 1840
MAF 32:	Ministry of Food: National Farm Survey, Individual Farm Records
MAF 48:	Agriculture, Fisheries and Food departments and related bodies, land correspondence and papers
MAF 174:	Ministry of Agriculture and Fisheries and Ministry of Agriculture, Fisheries and Food: Worcester Divisional Office: registered files
PROB 11:	Records of the Prerogative Court of Canterbury, registers of wills proved 1384–1858
RG 9–14:	General Register Office, Census Enumerators' returns 1861–1911

SC 6/HENVIII/1511:   Special Collections, Ministers' and Receivers Accounts for
                       estates in the possession of the Crown, Colwall, 1536–8

Worcestershire Archive and Archaeology Service at The Hive, Worcester holds the
records of Messrs. W. James, builders and contractors of Upper Colwall as well as some
other sources relevant to the history of Colwall.

Printed Sources

Primary Sources

The most important printed primary sources, including calendars of major classes in the
National Archives, are included in the List of Abbreviations.

The Registers of Bishops Cantilupe, Orleton, Thomas and Lewis Charlton, Trillek,
Courtenay, Gilbert, Trefnant, Mascall, Lacy, Polton, Spofford, Beauchamp, Boulers,
Stanbury, Milling, Mayew and Booth, which were printed by the Cantilupe Society
between 1906 and 1921, contain information about Colwall manor as well as the church.

Other published primary sources used in this history are:
> *English Episcopal Acta XXXV. Hereford 1234–75*, ed. J. Barrow (London, 2009).
> *Calendar of Probate and Administrative Acts 1407–1550 in the Consistory Court of the
> Bishops of Hereford*, ed. M.A. Faraday (Logaston, 2008).
> *Herefordshire Militia Assessments of 1663*, ed. M.A. Faraday, Camden 4th sers, X
> (1972).
> *Herefordshire Taxes in the reign of Henry VIII*, ed. M.A. Faraday (Hereford, 2005).
> *The Herefordshire Chantry Valuations of 1547*, ed. M.A. Faraday (privately
> printed, 2012).
> *Roll of the Household Expenses of Richard de Swinfield bishop of Hereford during part
> of the year 1289 and 1290*, ed. J. Webb, Camden Society, old sers, LIX, LXII (1854–5).

The tithe maps for all Herefordshire parishes including Colwall, have been privately
published by Geoff Gwatkin. Copies of the maps, which incorporate place-names
and other information concerning land use from the tithe awards, are available in
Herefordshire libraries and at HARC.

Trade or commercial directories have been used extensively. The main directories
consulted are: *Lascelles* (1851), *Littlebury's* (1876–7), *Kelly's* and *Jakeman's*. Many are
available online at http://specialcollections.le.ac.uk/cdm/landingpage/collection/
p16445coll4; others are to be found in the Herefordshire Archive Services' Library and
the Herefordshire Libraries collections.

The Woolhope Naturalists' Field Club (Archaeological Research Section) Herefordshire
Field-Name Survey based on the tithe maps provides a published list of field names by
parish. The field number and name is given. Colwall is parish number 145 and is based
on the apportionment of 1840 and 1842 map.

Secondary Sources

The most important secondary works on the history of Colwall are S. Ballard, *Colwall Collection: Memories of a Herefordshire Village* (Malvern, 1999) and Marjorie Thomas's unpublished 'History of Colwall' produced by Worcestershire Libraries. Brian S. Smith's, *A History of Malvern* (Leicester, 1964) also includes material relating to Colwall.

Two 19th-century works on Herefordshire history have been used: M.G. Watkins, *Collections for the History and Antiquities of Herefordshire*, Radlow Hundred (1902, bound as Duncomb's Herefordshire vol. 5) and C.J. Robinson, *A History of The Mansions and Manors of Herefordshire* (1873, reprinted Logaston, 2001). Also relevant are two 19th-century works on the Malvern Hills: E. Lees, *The Botany of the Malvern Hills* (Malvern, 1843) and *The Forest and Chace of Malvern, its Ancient & Present State; with notices of the most remarkable old trees remaining within its confines. Reprinted from the Transactions of the Malvern Naturalists' Field Club* (Worcester, 1877).

The main sources for architectural history are A. Brooks and N. Pevsner, *Herefordshire* (2012) and Royal Commission on Historical Monuments of England, *An Inventory of the Historical Monuments in Herefordshire*, II: East Herefordshire (1932).

Several works concerning the Malvern Hills contain information about Colwall including M. Bowden *The Malvern Hills: An Ancient Landscape* (Swindon, 2005, 2009) and P. Hurle, *The Forest and Chase of Malvern* (Chichester, 2007).

For place names in Herefordshire, see Bruce Coplestone-Crow, *Herefordshire Place-names* (Little Logaston, 2009).

For biographies of notable Herefordshire people, see P. Weaver, *A Dictionary of Herefordshire Biography* (Little Logaston 2015).

Websites

The Herefordshire Field-Name and Landowners Database provides the Herefordshire Field-Name Survey information online with the addition of landowner names extracted from the apportionments by Geoff Gwatkin: https://htt.herefordshire.gov.uk/her-search/field-names-and-landowners/.

A Vision of Britain through Time: http://www.visionofbritain.org.uk

British History Online: http://www.british-history.ac.uk

Clergy of the Church of England database: http://theclergydatabase.org.uk

Historic England's Red Box Collection: https://historicengland.org.uk/images-books/photos/englands-places/

Alumni Cantab.	*Alumni Cantabrigienses 1752–1900*, ed. J.A. Venn, 6 vols. (Cambridge, 1940–54)
Alumni Oxon.	*Alumni Oxonienses 1500–1714*, ed. J. Foster, 4 vols. (Oxford, 1891–2); *1715–1886*, 4 vols (Oxford, 1887–8)
BA	Bristol Archives
BL	British Library
Ballard, *Colwall Collection*	Stephen Ballard, *Colwall Collection: Memories of a Herefordshire Village* (Malvern, 1999)
Brooks and Pevsner, *Herefs.*	A. Brooks and N. Pevsner, *Herefordshire* (The Buildings of England, 2012)
Cal. Fine R.	*Calendar of the Fine Rolls preserved in the Public Record Office* (HMSO, 1903–27)
Cal. Inq. Misc.	*Calendar of Inquisitions Miscellaneous (Chancery) preserved in the Public Record Office* (HMSO, 1911–62)
Cal. Inq. p.m.	*Calendar of Inquisitions post mortem preserved in the Public Record Office* (HMSO, 1904–2010)
Cal. Papal Reg.	*Calendar of the Papal Registers: Papal Letters* (HMSO and Irish MSS. Com. 1891–2005)
Cal. Pat.	*Calendar of the Patent Rolls preserved in the Public Record Office* (HMSO, 1890–1986)
Cal. S.P. Dom.	*Calendar of State Papers, Domestic Series* (HMSO, 1856–1972)
CCED	*The Clergy of the Church of England Database*, http://theclergydatabase.org.uk
CERC	Church of England Record Centre
Colwall Clock	Colwall parish newsletter, available at Colwall Library
Crockford's Clerical Dir.	*Crockford's Clerical Directory*
CVS	Colwall Village Society
DCA	Dean and Chapter Archives, at Hereford Cathedral Library, Hereford
Domesday	A. Williams and G.H. Martin (eds), *Domesday Book: a Complete Translation* (London, 2002)

Dugdale, *Mon.*	W. Dugdale, *Monasticon Anglicanum*, ed. John Caley et al, 6 vols (1846–9)
Expenses of Swinfield	*Roll of the Household Expenses of Richard de Swinfield bishop of Hereford during part of the years 1289 and 1290*, ed. John Webb, Camden Soc. old sers. LIX, LXII (1854–5)
Fasti Eccles. Ang.	*Fasti Ecclesiae Anglicanae*
GA	Gloucestershire Archives
Goodbury, *Light on the Hill*	V. Goodbury, *A Light on the Hill – The Wyche Free Church* (2006)
HAS	Herefordshire Archive Service
HER	Historic Environment Record (formerly SMR or Sites and Monuments Record) at *Herefordshire Through Time*, http://htt.herefordshire.gov.uk
Heref. Institutions	*Diocese of Herefordshire Institutions, 1539–1900*, ed. A.T. Bannister (Hereford, 1923)
Herefs. Militia Assessments	*Herefs. Militia Assessments of 1663*, ed. M.A. Faraday, Camden 4th sers. X (1972)
Herefs. Taxes	*Herefs. Taxes in the Reign of Henry VIII, ed. M.A. Faraday (Heref. 2005)*
Hist. Parl.	*History of Parliament*
Hurle, *The Elms*	P. Hurle, *Portrait of a School: The Elms in Colwall, 1614–2000* (Colwall, 2000)
Hurle, *Forest and Chase*	P. Hurle, *The Forest and Chase of Malvern* (Chichester, 2007)
Hurle, *The Malvern Hills*	P. Hurle, *The Malvern Hills: A 100 years of Conservation* (Chichester, 1984)
Hurle, *Stephen Ballard*	P. Hurle, *Stephen Ballard, 1804–90: One of Nature's Gentlemen* (2010)
Inq. Non. (Rec. Com.)	*Nonarum Inquisitiones in Curia Scaccarii*, ed. G. Vandersee (Rec. Com. 1807)
L&P Hen. VIII	*Letters and Papers, Foreign and Domestic, of the Reign of Henry VIII* (HMSO, 1864–1932)
LPL	Lambeth Palace Library
MHC	Malvern Hills Conservators
NHLE	*National Heritage Listing for England*, http://www.historicengland.org.uk/listing/the-list
ODNB	*Oxford Dictionary of National Biography* (Oxford, 2004)
OS	Ordnance Survey
PAS	The Portable Antiquities Scheme, https://finds.org.uk
PastScape	*PastScape*, https://www.pastscape.org.uk

Pinches, *Ledbury: a Market Town*	S. Pinches, *Ledbury: A Market Town and its Tudor Heritage* (Chichester, 2009)
Pinches, *Ledbury: People and Parish*	S. Pinches, *Ledbury: People and Parish Before the Reformation* (Chichester, 2010)
Poll Taxes 1377–81, ed. Fenwick	*The Poll Taxes of 1377, 1379 and 1381, Part 1*, ed. Carolyn C. Fenwick (1998)
RCHME, *Inventory*	Royal Commission on Historical Monuments of England, *An Inventory of the Historical Monuments in Herefordshire*, 3 vols (1931–4)
'The Red Book', ed. Bannister	'A Transcript of "The Red Book"', ed. A.T. Bannister, *Camden Miscellany XV*, Camden Soc. 3rd ser. XLI (1929)
Rec. Com.	Record Commission
Reg. Bothe	*Registrum Caroli Bothe, episcopi Herefordensis 1516–1535*, ed. A.T. Bannister (Canterbury & York Society, 28, 1921)
Reg. Cantilupe	*Registrum Thome de Cantilupe, episcopi Herefordensis 1275–1282*, ed. W.W. Capes (Canterbury & York Society, 2, 1907)
Reg. Gilbert	*Registrum Johannis Gilbert, episcopi Herefordensis 1375–1389*, ed. J.H. Parry (Canterbury & York Society, 18, 1915)
Reg. Mascall	*Registrum Roberti Mascall, episcopi Herefordensis 1404–1416*, ed. J.H. Parry (Canterbury & York Society, 21, 1917)
Reg. Mayew	*Registrum Ricardi Mayew, episcopi Herefordensis 1504–1516*, ed. A.T. Bannister (Canterbury & York Society, 27, 1921)
Reg. Myllying	*Registrum Thome Myllying, episcopi Herefordensis 1474–1492*, ed. A.T. Bannister (Canterbury & York Society, 26, 1920)
Reg. Orleton	*Registrum Ade de Orleton, episcopi Herefordensis 1317–27*, ed. A.T. Bannister (Canterbury & York Society, 5, 1908)
Reg. Poltone	*Registrum Thome Poltone, episcopi Herefordensis 1420–1422*, ed. W.W. Capes (Canterbury & York Society, 22, 1918)
Reg. Spofford	*Registrum Thome Spofford, episcopi Herefordensis 1422–1448*, ed. A.T. Bannister (Canterbury & York Society, 23, 1919)
Reg. Stanbury	*Registrum Johannis Stanbury, episcopi Herefordensis 1453–1474*, ed. J.H. Parry (Canterbury & York Society, 25, 1919)

Reg. Swinfield	*Registrum Ricardi de Swinfield, episcopi Herefordensis 1283–1317,* ed. W.W. Capes (Canterbury & York Society, 6, 1909)
Reg. Thomas Charlton	*Registrum Thome de Charlton, episcopi Herefordensis 1327–1344* ed. W.W. Capes (Canterbury & York Society, 9, 1913)
Reg. Trefnant	*Registrum Johannis Trefnant, episcopi Herefordensis 1389–1404,* ed. W.W. Capes (Canterbury & York Society, 20, 1916)
Smith, *Malvern*	B. Smith, *A History of Malvern* (Leicester, 1964)
Tax. Eccles. (Rec. Com.)	*Taxatio Ecclesiastica Angliae et Walliae auctoritate P. Nicholai IV circa A.D. 1291, ed.* T. Astle, S. Ayscough, and J. Caley (Rec. Com. 1802)
TNA	The National Archives
TWNFC	*Transactions of the Woolhope Naturalists' Field Club*
Valor Eccl.	*Valor Ecclesiasticus temp. Hen. VIII auctoritate regia Institutus, ed.* J. Caley and J. Hunter (Rec. Com. 1810–34)
VCH Herefs. Bosbury	J. Cooper, *The Victoria History of Herefordshire: Bosbury* (2016)
VCH Herefs. Eastnor	J. Cooper, *The Victoria History of Herefordshire: Eastnor* (2013)
WAAS	Worcestershire Archives and Archaeological Service

THE FOLLOWING TERMS MAY REQUIRE explanation. Fuller information on local history topics is available in D.G. Hey, The Oxford Companion to Local and Family History (2nd edn, Oxford, 2010), or online from the VCH website https://www.history.ac.uk/research/victoria-county-history. The most convenient glossary of architectural terms is Pevsner's Architectural Glossary (2010), now also available in digital editions.

bay: in architecture, a unit of a building inside or out regularly divided from the next by features such as columns or windows. Can apply to a window projecting from a bay.

beerhouse: a public house licensed to sell beer but not spirits.

Black Death: outbreak of bubonic plague which killed about a third of the population of England in 1348–9.

bordar: cottager or peasant with lower economic status than a villein.

common (open) fields: communal agrarian organisation under which an individual's farmland was held in strips scattered amongst two or more large fields, intermingled with strips of other tenants. Management of the fields and usually common meadows and pasture was regulated through the manor court or other communal assembly.

copyhold: form of land tenure granted in a manor court, so called because the tenant received a 'copy' of the grant as noted in the court records. Often given for several lives (e.g. tenant, wife, and eldest child).

customary tenure: unfree or copyhold tenure regulated by local manorial custom.

demesne: in the Middle Ages, land farmed directly by a lord of the manor, rather than granted to tenants. Though usually leased out from the later Middle Ages, demesne lands often remained distinct from the rest of a parish's land.

dey-house: a dairy house.

glebe: land assigned to the rector or vicar of a church for his support and the endowment of the church.

haia: a hedged enclosure designed for the capture of wild animals, usually deer, during the hunt.

hearth tax: annual tax imposed by central government in 1662–89, assessed on the number of hearths or fireplaces in each house and payable by the occupier. Those who lacked the means to pay could apply for a certificate of exemption.

hide: unit of land measurement: in the Anglo-Saxon period the amount required for a family to subsist on; in Domesday Book (1086), a taxation unit; and by the 13th century the sum of 4 yardlands (q.v.).

manor: a piece of landed property with tenants regulated by a private (manor) court. Originally held by feudal tenure, manors descended through a succession of heir buts could be given away or sold.

messuage: portion of land or holding, generally with a house and outbuildings on it.

parish: the area attached to a parish church and owing tithe to it. From the Elizabethan period it had civil responsibilities, hence a 'civil' as opposed to an 'ecclesiastical' parish. At first the two were usually identical, but from the 19th century, when many parishes were reorganised, their boundaries sometimes diverged.

patron (of a church): the person having the right to nominate a candidate to the bishop for appointment as rector or vicar of a church. Often the lord of the manor, but the right could be bought and sold.

ploughland: notionally the amount of land a plough team of eight oxen could plough in a season.

prebend: land or other property (including tithes) owned by a cathedral, and allocated in perpetuity to one of the cathedral's canon (or 'prebendaries').

radman: a feudal tenant who held land on condition of performing service for the lord on horseback.

rectory: (a) a church living served by a rector, who generally received the church's whole income; (b) the church's property or endowment (the rectory estate), comprising tithes, offerings, and usually some land or glebe.

vestry: (a) in a church where clerical vestments are stored; (b) assembly of leading parishioners and ratepayers, responsible for poor relief and other secular matters as well as church affairs.

villeins: feudal tenants that were entirely subject to the lord or manor to whom he paid dues and services in return for land.

yardland: the conventional holding of a medieval peasant, of 15–40 acres depending on local custom. Most generated surplus crops for sale at market, although those with fragments of yardlands probably needed to work part-time for better-off neighbours.

yeoman: from the 16th century, a term used for more prosperous farmers, many of them socially aspirational. The term husbandman usually denoted less well-off farmers.

Rectors of Colwall until 1840

Name of priest	Year	Source
Adam the priest	fl. 1171 x 1178	Dugdale, *Mon.* IV, 449–50; *VCH Warks.* V, 190
Walter of Colwall	fl. 1179 x 1186	Fasti Eccles. Ang. 1066–1300, VIII, 92
Gerard of Eugines	fl. 1276	*Reg. Cantilupe*, 86
John de Clare	1279–83	*Reg. Cantilupe*, lxx–lxxi, 195–6
John de Kempsey	1283–c.1297	*Reg. Cantilupe*, lxx–lxxi; *Reg. Swinfield*, v, 524; *Fasti Eccles. Ang. 1300–1541*, II, 10, 18
Richard de Kyngesnode	c.1297–c.1313	*Cal. Pat. 1292–1301*, 278; *Reg. Swinfield*, 546
Robert de la Felde	fl. 1330	*Cal. Papal Reg. 1305–42*, 332; *Reg. Thomas Charlton*, 90
Elias de Blakeney	fl. 1344–6	*Reg. Trillek*, 395
John Staunton	?–1378	*Reg. Gilbert*, 115
Nicholas Bacon	1378–80	*Reg. Gilbert*, 115, 122
William Horeworth	1380–94	*Reg. Gilbert*, 122; *Reg. Trefnant*, 179, 189
John Hampton	1394–1400	*Reg. Trefnant*, 179, 184, 189
Richard Coylying	1400–1	*Reg. Trefnant*, 184
Benedict Edine	fl. 1401	*Reg. Trefnant*, 185
Thomas Kellet	1415–21	*Reg. Mascall*, 85
John Pyd	1421–3	*Reg. Poltone*, 16; *Reg. Spofford*, 351
Richard Carpenter	1423–7	*Reg. Spofford*, 351, 353
William Ward	1427–?	*Reg. Spofford*, 353
John Dylew	?–1443	*Reg. Spofford*, 242, 249, 251, 364
John Clone	1443–8	*Reg. Spofford*, 251, 364
John Dylew	1448–c.1452	*Reg. Spofford*, 368
John Clone	c.1452–63	*Reg. Boulers*, 23; Emden, *Register of the University of Oxford*, I, 566–7
Richard Jaxone	?–1466	*Reg. Stanbury*, 182
Thomas Hall	1466–92	*Reg. Stanbury*, 179–80, 182
Robert Asplin	1492–1515	*Reg. Myllying*, 201, 207

John Viall	1515–25	*Reg. Mayew*, 284, 290; *Fasti Eccles. Ang. 1300–1541*, II, 40,48
Hugh Charnock	1525–51	*Reg. Bothe*, 338; *CCED*, no. 169855; *Alumni Oxon. 1500–1714*, 264; *Fasti Eccles. Ang. 1300–1541*, II, 44
John Styrmyne	1551–2	*CCED*, no. 90365; *Heref. Institutions*, 7–8
William Chelle	1552–7	*Fasti Eccles. Ang. 1300–1541*, II, 22; *1541–1857*, XIII, 16, 44, 51; *Alumni Oxon. 1500–1714, 266*; *ODNB*, s.v. Chelle, William, Church of England clergyman and musician (accessed 30 Sept. 2019)
Henry Tanner	1557–75	*CCED*, no. 65296; *Heref. Institutions*, 12; *Fasti Heref.* 95; *Alumni Oxon. 1500–1714*, 1455; *Fasti Eccles. Ang. 1541–1857*, XIII, 108
Richard Barnard alias Nicholas	1575–c.1623	*CCED*, no. 169024; *Heref. Institutions*, 23
John Haylings	*c.*1623–*c.*1670	*CCED*, no. 171676; HAS, 33/2/52, will of John Rowberry, 1623; 26/1/50, will of Anne Halings, 1670
John Page	1673–97	*Heref. Institutions*, 39; *CCED*, no. 173040
Charles Whiting	1697–99	*Heref. Institutions*, 55; *CCED*, no. 174474; *Alumni Oxon. 1500–1714*, 1621; *Fasti Eccles. Ang. 1541–1857*, XIII, 118, 135
John Page	1699–1723	*CCED*, no. 173042; *Heref. Institutions*, 56; *Alumni Oxon. 1500–1714*, 1105; *Fasti Eccles. Ang. 1541–1857*, XIII, 109
William Stevenson	1723–47	*Heref. Institutions*, 70
Thomas Hensleigh	1747–62	*Heref. Institutions*, 86; *CCED*, no. 68643; *Alumni Oxon. 1715–1886*, 647
John Stephens	1762–3	CCED, no. 165088; Heref. Institutions, 96; Fasti Eccles. Ang. 1541–1857, XIII, 99; Fasti. Heref. 106
Uvedale Kyffin	1763–77	*CCED*, no. 34844; *Heref. Institutions*, 97; *Alumni Oxon. 1715–1886*, 807; *Fasti Eccles. Ang. 1541–1857*, XIII, 43, 87
William Reece	1777–81	*Heref. Institutions*, 109
Joseph Taylor	1781–3	*Heref. Institutions*, 113; *CCED*, no. 174090
James Charles Clarke	1783–1831	*Heref. Institutions*, 119
Thomas Wynne	1831–9	*CCED*, no. 22038; *Heref. Institutions*, 150; *Alumni Oxon. 1715–1886*, 1621
William Peete Musgrave	1839–40	*Alumni Cantab. 1752–1900*, IV, 505

INDEX

Italicised page numbers refer to illustrations on that page.

CPSIA information can be obtained
at www.ICGtesting.com
Printed in the USA
JSHW010030010421
13027JS00008B/48

9 781912 702077